OCR Level 2 ITQ

Unit 59
Presentation Software

Using
Microsoft® PowerPoint 2010

Release ITQOCR26v1

Published by:

CiA Training Ltd
Business & Innovation Centre
Sunderland Enterprise Park
Sunderland
SR5 2TA
United Kingdom

Tel: +44 (0) 191 549 5002
Fax: +44 (0) 191 549 9005

E-mail: info@ciatraining.co.uk
Web: www.ciatraining.co.uk

ISBN: 978-1-86005-908-7

Important Notes

This guide was written for *Microsoft Office 2010* running on *Windows 7*. If using a different version of *Windows* some dialog boxes may look and function slightly differently to that described. It is also assumed file extensions are enabled in *Windows*, which is important for demonstrating the differences between file types.

To turn on file extensions, click the **Start** button and open the **Control Panel**. From **Appearance and Personalization** select **Folder Options**, and then from the dialog box click the **View** tab and uncheck **Hide extensions for known file types**. Click **OK**.

A resolution of *1024x768* was also used to produce screenshots for this guide. Working at a different resolution (or with an application window which is not maximised) may change the look of the dynamic *Office Ribbon*, which changes to fit the space available.

 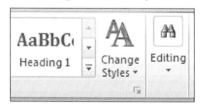

For example, the **Editing Group** on a full *Ribbon* will contain several buttons, but if space is restricted it may be replaced by an **Editing Button** (which, when clicked, will display the full **Editing Group**).

First published 2011

Overview of the unit

This level 2 unit is called **Presentation Software** and requires you to make best use of presentation software to produce presentations. It has a credit value of **4**.

At this level you are required to demonstrate the skills and techniques necessary to use a range of intermediate presentation software tools to create, format and run presentations. Any aspect that is unfamiliar to you may require support and advice from others.

This guide is designed to be used with *Microsoft PowerPoint 2010* and contains exercises covering the following topics:

- Open & Close Presentations
- Saving Presentations
- Views
- Bullet Levels
- Adding Slides
- Text Formatting & Effects
- Automatic Fields
- Find & Replace
- Organisation Charts

- Master Slides
- Inserting & Manipulating Pictures
- Inserting Tables & Charts
- Action Buttons & Hyperlinks
- Animation Effects
- Slide Transitions & Timings
- Running Presentations
- Speaker's Notes
- Printing of Presentations

Software and data files

Microsoft PowerPoint 2010 is part of the *Microsoft Office* 2010 suite of applications. This guide assumes that the program has been fully installed on your computer. Some features described in this guide may not work correctly if the program was not fully installed.

Downloadable data accompanying this guide contains files to enable you to practise new techniques without the need for data entry. Newly created files can be saved to the same location.

Downloading the Data Files

The data files associated with this guide must be downloaded from our website. To do this, go to **www.ciatraining.co.uk/data** and follow the simple on-screen instructions.

Your *FastCode* for this guide's data is: **ITQOCR26**

The data will be installed to the following location in your **Documents** library\folder:

DATA FILES \ OCR Level 2 ITQ \ Unit 59 PowerPoint 2010

If you prefer, the data files can also be supplied on CD at an additional cost. Contact the Sales team at info@ciatraining.co.uk.

Aims and objectives

The purpose of this guide is to provide the knowledge and techniques necessary to meet the learning outcomes and assessment criteria for this optional unit.

After completing this guide you will be able to:

- Use appropriate software to create a presentation

- Set up master slide layout in accordance with a specified house style

- Import, insert and manipulate data/graphics/slides

- Add animations, sound and video to slides

- Control a presentation using timings and transitions

- Print presentations and support documents

Notation used throughout this guide

- Key presses are included within angled brackets. For example, <**Enter**> means press the **Enter** key.

- The guide is split into individual exercises. Each exercise usually consists of a written explanation of a specific learning outcome (Knowledge), followed by a stepped exercise (Activity).

Recommendations

- Work through the exercises in sequence so that one feature is understood before moving on to the next.

- Read the whole of each exercise before starting to work through it. This ensures understanding of the topic and prevents unnecessary mistakes.

This guide is suitable for:

- Any individual wishing to gain the skills necessary to produce ITQ (2009) evidence for this unit. The user should work through the guide from start to finish. Some prior knowledge of *PowerPoint 2010* (to Level 1 standard) would be useful.

- Tutor led groups as reinforcement material. It can be used as and when necessary.

Skill Check

After you have finished working through each Skill Set, come back to this checklist and review your progress. You judge when you are competent – only when you fully understand the learning aims of each exercise topic should you progress to the next Skill Set.

1: No Knowledge **2**: Some Knowledge **3**: Competent

Skill Set	No	Exercise	1	2	3
1 Basics	1	Presentations			
	2	Creating a New Presentation			
	3	Saving a Presentation			
	4	Closing a Presentation			
	5	Opening a Presentation			
2 Presentation Styles	7	Themes			
	8	Colour Schemes			
	9	Using Slide Master			
	10	Formatting Slide Master			
	11	Bullet Levels			
	12	Adding Automatic Fields			
	13	Applying a Background			
3 Templates	15	Using an Existing Template			
	16	Creating a Template			
	17	Amending a Template			
	18	Using a Created Template			
	19	Apply a Saved Theme			
4 Editing Content	21	Using Undo and Redo			
	22	Using Copy and Paste			
	23	Using Cut and Paste			
	24	Importing text			
	25	Inserting Text			
	26	Find and Replace Data			

1: No Knowledge **2**: Some Knowledge **3**: Competent

Skill Set	No	Exercise	1	2	3
5 PowerPoint Objects	28	Inserting a Diagram			
	29	Organisation Charts			
	30	Formatting Organisation Charts			
	31	Inserting Clip Art			
	32	Moving and resizing Objects			
	33	Object Orientation			
	34	Objects on Slide Master			
	35	Inserting a Picture from File			
	36	Cropping a Picture			
	37	Aligning Data with Tabs			
	38	Tables			
	39	Inserting Charts			
	40	Formatting Charts			
6 Controlling a Presentation	42	Changing Slide Order			
	43	Deleting Slides			
	44	Hiding Slides			
	45	Hyperlinks			
	46	Action Buttons			
	47	Using Built-In Animation			
	48	Using Custom Animation			
	49	Animating Charts			
	50	Setting Up a Slide Show			
	51	Adding Sound			
	52	Adding a Movie			
	53	Applying Slide Transitions			
	54	Applying Timings			
	55	Rehearse Timings			
7 Finishing and Printing	57	Adding Speaker's Notes			
	58	Start and End Slides			
	59	Spell Checking			
	60	Proof Reading			
	61	Page Setup			
	62	Printing Slides and Presentations			
	63	Other Prints			

Contents

Skill Set 1

Basics

By the end of this Skill Set you should be able to:

Create a New Presentation

Save a Presentation

Close a Presentation

Open a Presentation

Switch between Views

Exercise 1 - Presentations

Knowledge:

A presentation is a way of displaying information about a topic by using a series of single-screen "slides". It can be shown on a computer screen, an overhead projector, as 35mm slides, or as web pages. The presentation can be given by a presenter who will control the display of the slides, or it can be left to run automatically.

Because of the nature of a presentation (single screens, possibly shown to a large audience) it usually relies heavily on visual impact rather than textual content. So a typical slide will have limited, summarised text, often in the form of bullet points, or graphic content in the form of images, animations, charts, etc.

It follows then that colour and style are very important issues. Visual impact is almost everything in a presentation. You should be aware of the value of using pictures rather than too much text and using charts rather than rows of figures. You should also be aware of the emotional implications of certain colours and colour schemes, such as reds being stimulating and representing energy and danger, while blues are associated with calmness and stability. The use of colours is quite a large subject and there are several Internet web sites that can provide information at many levels.

There are also more practical implications of using colour with regard to clarity. Some people have difficulty separating certain colour combinations, commonly red-green, so be careful when using these combinations to convey data. Also, always ensure a good contrast between text colour and background colour so that the text is clear, even when the presentation is given in a large room.

In general, don't use too many different colours, styles or effects in the same presentation as the clarity of the message may be obscured. A simple consistent design scheme is usually more effective. In many organisations this is forced on the designer by the use of a defined "house style" (a set of consistent design styles that reflects the look of the business – fonts, logos, colours, etc.), which must be used for all presentations.

Other factors can affect the design of the presentation. Always consider the actual purpose of the presentation. If it is to promote your company to potential *investors* then it may have a different style to a presentation created to advertise your company to potential *customers*. The final form of the presentation may also have an effect; a presentation intended to run on a big screen in a hall may need different design features to one which will run on a small screen.

Exercise 2 - Creating a New Presentation

Knowledge:

There are various options available to you when starting a new presentation.

- A blank presentation can be started, without colours, background or graphics.

- A presentation can be created based on an existing template. Templates will be covered in a later exercise.

- An existing presentation can be opened, amended, and then saved with a new name.

This exercise will start an unformatted blank presentation.

Activity:

1. Start *PowerPoint* by clicking on the **Start** button, and then **All Programs**. Click once on the **Microsoft Office** folder and then **Microsoft PowerPoint 2010**.

2. *PowerPoint* starts with a new blank presentation.

> **Note:** *To start a new, blank presentation at any time, click the **File** tab and select **New** with **Blank presentation** selected click **Create**.*

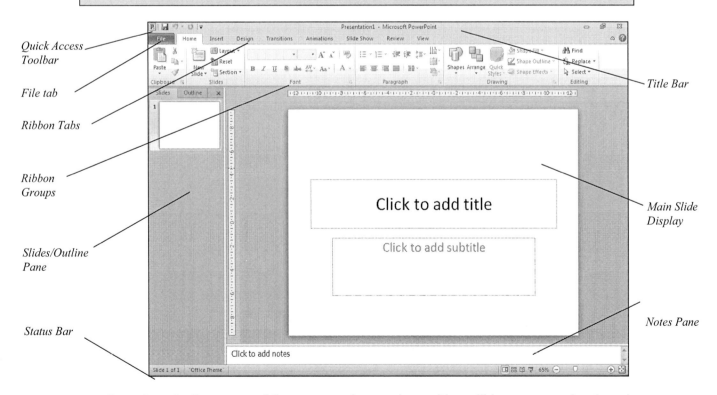

3. Locate the areas of the screen shown above. You will learn more about each feature as you progress through this guide.

Exercise 2 - Continued

> **Note:** *The presentation will be given a temporary name of **Presentation1** (shown on the application's **Title Bar**) until it is saved for the first time.*

4. The first blank slide of the presentation is displayed in the centre of the application window, with the **Slides** pane on the left.

> **Note:** *The view on screen is known as the **Normal** view. You will learn more about different views in another exercise.*

5. A **Title Slide** layout has been selected by default. Click the **Layout** button, Layout ▾ , within the **Slides** group on the **Home** tab.

6. Select a few of the different layouts in turn and see how the view in the main **Slide** pane changes.

7. Finally select the first layout, **Title Slide**.

8. A presentation to help recruit new staff to a high technology company is to be created. Click on the slide where indicated to add a title, and type **Far North Technologies**.

9. Click in the box below to add a subtitle, and type **A Fresh Start**.

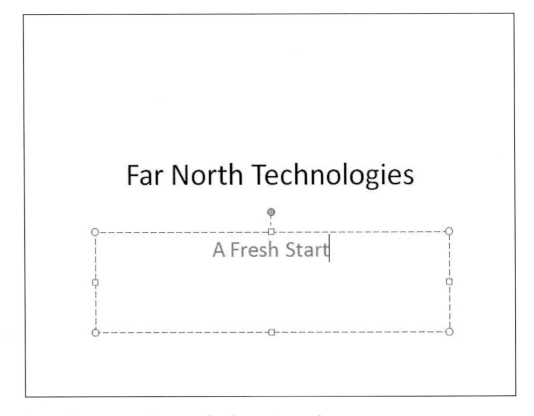

10. Leave the presentation open for the next exercise.

Exercise 3 - Saving a Presentation

Knowledge:

A presentation must be saved if it is to be used again. The **Save As** command will always prompt for a file name, a location where the file will be stored, and a file type. For a file that has been saved already, the **Save** command will save the file with the same name, location and type that it had when it was opened (and will overwrite the original version).

Activity:

1. The presentation created in the previous exercise should still be on screen. Click the **File** tab and select **Save As**. The **Save As** dialog box will then appear with default values for location, file name and file type (the contents of the dialog box may be different to those shown below).

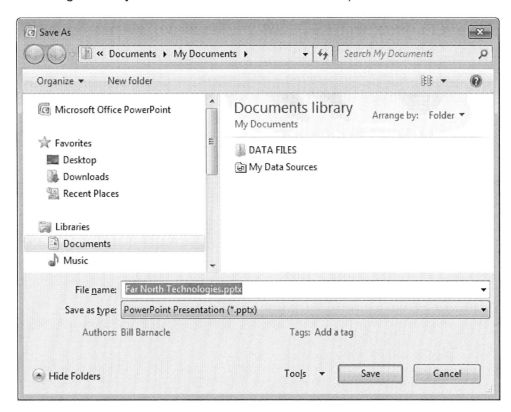

2. Use the **Save in** box to locate the folder where you want to store the file. For this exercise the folder containing the downloaded data files for this course will be used (see *Downloading the Data Files* on page 3).

3. Double click on the **DATA FILES** folder, then **OCR Level 2 ITQ**, and finally **Unit 59 PowerPoint 2010**. The data files used for this unit are now listed.

> **Note:**   *To save the current presentation, it must be given a suitable file name.*

4. Enter **far north** in the **File name** box (the highlighted text will automatically be replaced).

Exercise 3 - Continued

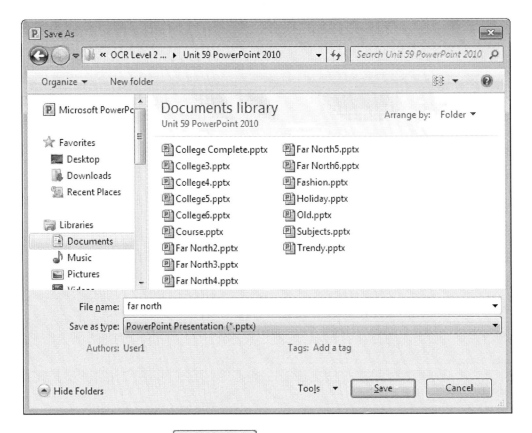

5.   Click the **Save** button, [Save], found towards the bottom right of the dialog box.

Note: *The file extension .pptx is added automatically.*

---

6.   Notice how the label on the **Title Bar** has changed to show the new file name.

7.   Leave the presentation on screen for the next exercise.

Note: *A previously named presentation can be saved to the same location under the same name by clicking the **Save** button,* ▦ *, on the **Quick Access Toolbar**. When a new presentation is to be saved, clicking **Save** displays the **Save As** dialog box.*

Exercise 4 - Closing a Presentation

Knowledge:

To clear the screen and begin working on a new presentation, the current one can be closed. If the presentation has not been previously saved, or if it has been modified in any way, a prompt to save it will appear.

Activity:

1. The **far north** presentation should still be on the screen. Change the subtitle text to read **A Fresh Career**. To close the presentation, click the **File** tab.

2. Click **Close** As changes have been made to the presentation since last saving, there will be a warning message prompting you to save the changes.

3. Click **Save** to save the changes. The presentation closes without any further prompt.

> **Note:** *If no changes had been made to the presentation since it was last saved, it would be closed without displaying the save prompt.*

Exercise 5 - Opening a Presentation

Knowledge:

Once created and saved, a presentation can be opened at any time.

Activity:

1. With no presentations open, click the **File** tab and select **Open**.

2. The **Open** dialog box appears. Make sure that the **File types** drop-down at the bottom right shows **All PowerPoint Presentations**.

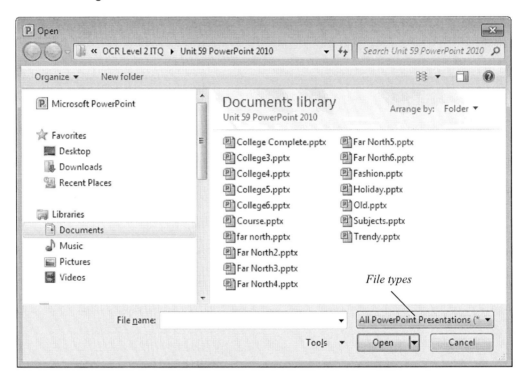

3. In the dialog box, the folder **Unit 59 PowerPoint 2010** should be displayed. If not, navigate to this location now.

4. Select **Holiday** from the list of files and click **Open**, ⬜ Open ▼ . The presentation opens in **Normal** view.

5. Slide **1** is shown in the centre of the screen. It is a **Title Slide** which shows a sound icon in the middle.

> **Note:** *The sound icon indicates that a sound will play when this presentation is run.*

6. Click on slide **2** in the **Slides** pane.

7. This is a **Title and Content** slide. With the **Home** tab displayed, click the **Layout** drop-down in the **Slides** group to confirm the slide layout type.

Exercise 5 - Continued

8.   Click away from the menu to close it.

9.   To display a later slide in the presentation, use the scroll bar in the **Slides** pane to view all available slides (scroll down to locate slide **10**, the final slide).

10.   Click on slide **8**. This slide contains a table.

11.   Click on slide **9**. This slide contains a chart.

12.   Click on slide **10** again. This slide has a different layout – find out what it is using the **Layout** button.

Note:	*It is a **Two Content** layout slide.*

13.   Use the **View** buttons, on the right of the **Status Bar** to view the presentation in **Slide Sorter** view.

Note:	***Slide Sorter** view allows you to reorder slide thumbnails. It is useful for previewing a presentation and to change the order, effects and timings of the slide show.*

14.   All ten slides are displayed. Look at the notations beneath each slide, 00:06 . The star denotes an animated transition from slide to slide and the number denotes the time each slide is on view, i.e. 6 seconds in each case.

15.   Click on slide **1**, as you are about to run the show from the beginning. The selected slide has an orange outline.

16.   This show has a sound attached, so – if available – make sure that your speakers are on but at a low volume.

17.   To view the show, which moves between slides automatically, click the **Slide Show** button, , to the right on the **Status Bar**.

18.   When the show ends a black screen is displayed. Click once to return to **Slide Sorter** view.

19.   Run the show again but this time click the mouse button when you want the slide to change.

Note:	*If you do not click within 6 seconds, the show will advance automatically.*

20.   Return to **Normal** view by selecting the **View** tab and selecting **Normal**.

Note:	***Normal** view is used to edit individual slides.*

21.   Close the presentation.

Exercise 6 - Develop Your Skills

You will find a *Develop Your Skills* exercise at the end of each Skill Set. Work through it to ensure you've understood the previous exercises.

1. Create a new blank presentation.

> **Hint:** *Click the **File** tab and select **New** with **Blank Presentation** selected click **Create**.*

2. Enter a title of **ITQ Sample** on the first slide.

3. Save the presentation as **sample1** in the same folder as the data that accompanies this guide.

4. Close the presentation.

5. Open the **Course** presentation from the data files.

6. Run the slide show. This presentation has been saved so that nothing needs to be done during the show.

7. If the show ends on a black slide, click once with the mouse to end the show.

8. Switch to **Slide Sorter** view.

9. Save the presentation as **course2**.

10. Switch back to **Normal** view.

11. Close the presentation.

12. Close *PowerPoint*.

> **Hint:** *Click the **File** tab and select **Close**.*

Summary: Basics

In this Skill Set you have started the presentation software program *PowerPoint*. You have opened, saved and closed presentations.

<u>Your OCR ITQ evidence must demonstrate your ability to:</u>

- Locate presentation files

- Open presentation files

- Create a new presentation:
    - Name presentations with appropriate names
    - Save new presentation using Save As in a recognised folder

- Close presentation files

Skill Set 2

Presentation Styles

By the end of this Skill Set you should be able to:

Use Themes

Amend Colour Schemes

Set up a Slide Master

Format a Slide Master

Use Different Bullet Levels

Insert Automatic Fields

Apply a Background

Exercise 7 - Themes

Knowledge:

More often than not, it is important for any presentation to have a consistent style across all slides. Although the same formatting can be copied manually to every slide in a presentation, *PowerPoint* offers several more efficient methods of doing this automatically. The quickest way is to apply a **Theme** to the presentation.

A **Theme** is a coordinated set of background colours, graphics, and text formatting definitions which can be applied to all slides in one go. Once applied, the design template characteristics can be altered manually to suit.

Activity:

1. Open the **Far North2** presentation from the supplied data files. This is the first three slides of a recruitment presentation with no formatting applied. Display slide **2** in **Normal** view.

2. Select the **Design** tab. The **Themes**, **Background** and **Page Setup** groups will be displayed.

3. Place your mouse pointer over some of the available theme thumbnails in the **Themes** group on the **Ribbon** (but do <u>not</u> click). A preview of how this theme will affect your presentation is shown. Notice how the background colours, graphics, bullet points and text formatting all change.

4. Click to select a theme of your choice. Notice that all slides in the presentation are changed, displayed in the **Slides** pane on the left.

5. Click the **More** drop-down arrow, ⊞, to the right of the theme icons, and select the theme called **Concourse** (the names of the themes will appear in a **ToolTip** as the mouse pointer hovers over the preview images).

> **Note:** *If this theme is not available on your computer, use an alternative.*

6. Save the presentation as **themed** and leave it open for the next exercise.

Exercise 8 - Colour Schemes

Knowledge:

Each *PowerPoint* theme includes a **colour scheme**. This is a set of coordinated colours which are applied – in different ways – to the various aspects of the presentation's design. It is easy to change the individual colours within a scheme.

Activity:

1. The **themed** presentation should be open with the **Concourse** theme applied and slide **2** displayed.

2. To change the current colour scheme, click **Colors**, 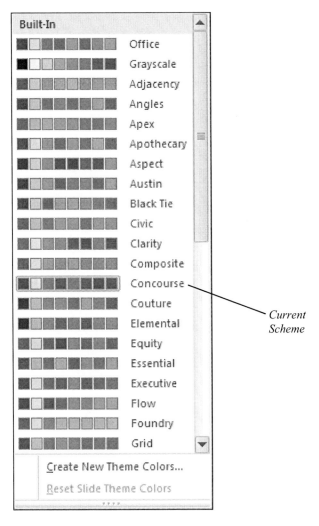, from the **Themes** group (on the **Design** tab). The currently selected colour scheme is highlighted with a border.

Current Scheme

3. Place your mouse pointer over some of the available schemes (but do <u>not</u> click). A preview of how this theme will affect your presentation is shown.

4. Select **Create New Theme Colors** from the bottom of the list.

Exercise 8 - Continued

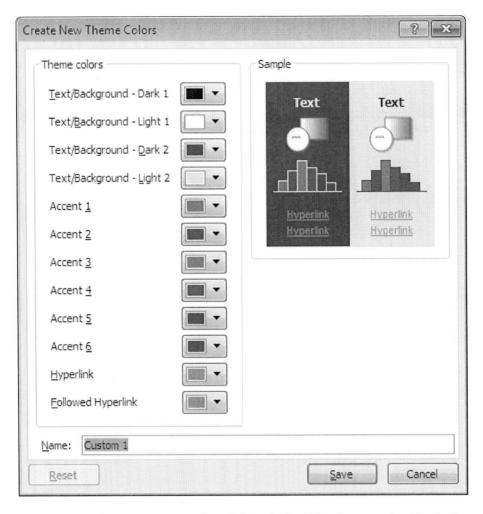

5. Click the drop-down arrow to the right of **Text/Background - Dark 2** and select a purple colour from **Standard Colors**.

6. Notice how the sample at the left (the darker sample) changes.

7. Change **Text/Background – Light 2** to green from **Standard Colors**.

8. To save the changes as a new theme, replace the text in the **Name** box with **My Theme** and click **Save**. The amended theme is applied to the presentation.

9. Click **Colors**, Colors ▾, again. Your selected colour scheme is shown towards the top of the list.

10. Now apply the **Paper** colour scheme from the **Built-In** colour options in the **Theme** group. The **Concourse** theme is still applied but with a different set of colours.

11. Leave the presentation open for the next exercise.

Exercise 9 - Using Slide Master

Knowledge:

The most efficient way to apply consistent design to a presentation is to use a feature called a **Slide Master**. This allows uniform background effects, text formatting and graphics to be added to every slide. Any effect added to the **Slide Master** will automatically affect all slides in the presentation. If a new slide is added, it will automatically display the **Slide Master** formatting.

The **Slide Master** is one of three different master pages that can be defined in *PowerPoint*, the others being **Handout Master** and **Notes Master**. Only **Slide Master** will be covered in this guide.

Activity:

1. Slide **2** of the **themed** presentation should still be displayed. Select the **View** tab and click **Slide Master**. The slide master is now shown.

> **Note:** *Layouts are used to define formatting and positioning of content in the presentation. The theme and layouts used are shown in the pane at the left.*

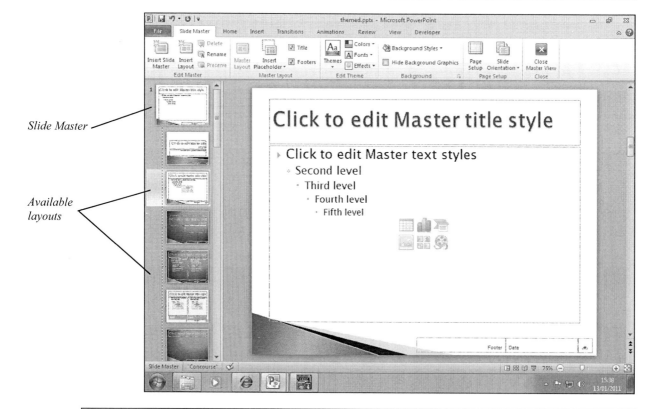

> **Note:** *Any changes made in this view will affect the whole presentation. For example, text or graphics added to this slide will appear on every slide in your presentation.*

2. Leave this view open for the next exercise.

Exercise 10 - Formatting Slide Master

Knowledge:

The **Slide Master** can be formatted using all of the techniques used for formatting any slides. This includes changing fonts, colours and alignment. The difference is that the formatting will be applied to all slides in the presentation and all slides that are added later.

Something to be aware of when formatting is the difference between **serif** and **sans serif** fonts. A **serif** font has curls, or tails, on the letter stalks, e.g. **h**, and a **sans serif** font does not, e.g. **h**.

Many organisations will define a single set of formatting (called a house style) which is to be applied to all presentations (and even letters and documents, etc.) within the organisation. This is intended to produce a consistent recognisable 'look' or corporate image to all the output from an organisation. House styles are ideally applied to the **Slide Master**

Activity:

1. The **themed** presentation **Slide Master** should still be open. Select the larger **Slide Master** at the top left of the pane (this is the main master slide).

2. Select all of the text **Click to edit Master title style**, as shown below.

> **Note:** The format of text can be changed while the cursor is within the text. Take care not to click on a space between words.

3. Display the **Home** tab.

> **Note:** Notice the font type, size and alignment selected.

Exercise 10 - Continued

4. The existing font is **Lucida Sans Unicode**; a **sans serif** font.

5. Assume that your employer's house style states that titles should be **Times New Roman** (a **serif** font), **44pt**, **Bold** and **Italic**. Change the font to **Times New Roman**, the font style to **Italic** and the size to **44** using the buttons in the **Font** group.

6. **Centre** the text, but leave other definitions such as the **Color** and the **Shadow** effect as they are.

Note:	Other parts of the slide can also be set to match your house style requirements.

7. Click within the top bullet text: **Click to edit Master text styles**, then change the font to **Arial** and the size to **28pt**. Leave the other settings.

8. Select the next bullet text: **Second Level**.

9. Set the font to **Arial**, the style to **Italic** and the size to **24pt**.

10. To change the font colour of this bullet, click the **Font Color** button drop-down and select a colour of your choice from within **Theme Colors**.

11. Click in the text **Click to edit Master title style** again. To add a border to this text box, click the **Quick Styles** button in the **Drawing** group. Select any style of your choice (the style second from the left on the top line is suitable).

12. To change the colour of the border, click the **Shape Outline** button in the **Drawing** group and select another colour of your choice.

Note:	The style of the border can be changed using the other options within **Shape Outline**. Borders can be added to any text box or object using these methods.

13. To remove the border, with the cursor in the box, click the **Shape Outline** button and select **No Outline**.

14. Display the **Slide Master** tab and click **Close Master View** to see how the presentation has been affected.

15. Leave the presentation open for the next exercise.

Exercise 11 - Bullet Levels

Knowledge:

Text that you enter on a slide often takes the form of **bullet points**. There are several levels of bulleted text available which allow minor details to be made about major points. The formatting of bullet points for the whole presentation can be set in **Slide Master** view. This includes the bullet symbols themselves.

When text is entered on a slide *PowerPoint* assumes that it will be a **first level** bullet point. The process of changing to a second level bullet is called **Demotion**. Conversely, if text is at second level and you decide that it is a main point, then it can be **Promoted**. These actions are carried out on the **Outline** pane at the left.

Activity:

1. The **themed** presentation should still be open. Change to **Slide Master** view and make sure the main slide master (the one at the top) is selected.

2. The first two levels are the only two that will concern you. Click in the **First level** bullet text (**Master text styles**). The bullet level fonts were changed in the previous exercise but other formatting can be amended.

3. Select the **Home** tab and click the **Line Spacing** button, .

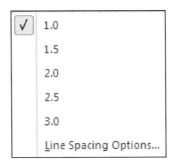

4. Select **1.5** lines. The first level bullet points will now be spaced further apart on the slides.

5. Bullet symbols can also be changed. Click the drop-down arrow on the **Bullets** button, , to display a list of options.

6. Select **Arrow Bullets**. The first level bullet symbol changes.

> **Note:**   An alternative method for changing the bullet symbol is to right click in the required level bullet text and select **Bullets**.

Exercise 11 - Continued

> **Note:** To further customise bullet symbols (and even choose your own pictures to use), click the **Bullets** drop-down arrow and select **Bullets and Numbering**. The **Picture** and **Customize** buttons can be used to tailor bullet points to suit your presentation.

7. Display the **Slide Master** tab and select **Close Master View**.

> **Note:** Notice that the text and bullets have changed to reflect the **Slide Master**.

8. Select slide **3** of the presentation. Notice that the text and bullets have been changed here also.

9. Display the **Outline** pane (by clicking [Outline] on the **Slides/Outline Pane**).

10. The slide **3** text is automatically selected. Click away to deselect it.

11. Click in the second bullet point, **First satellite launch in 1999**.

12. Click the **Increase List Level** button, in the **Paragraph** group on the Home tab. The text becomes second level and adopts the formatting defined for this level in the previous exercise.

13. In this case however, the bullets should all be first level. Click the **Decrease List Level** button, to promote the **Satellite** bullet back to first level.

> **Note:** These actions can also be achieved by right clicking on a bullet level and using **Promote** and **Demote** to move up and down the levels.

14. Redisplay the **Slides** pane (by clicking [Slides]).

15. Save the presentation and leave it open for the next exercise.

Exercise 12 - Adding Automatic Fields

Knowledge:

Items such as the date, the name of the designer, and the slide number can be added so that they appear on each slide in the presentation. The data can be added using **Header and Footer** view. By default the data is shown along the lower edge of each slide. If the date is inserted as an **automatic field**, it will update each time the presentation is opened, saved or printed.

Activity:

1.   View the slide **2** of the **themed** presentation.

2.   Select the **Insert** tab and click **Header & Footer** to display the **Header and Footer** dialog box.

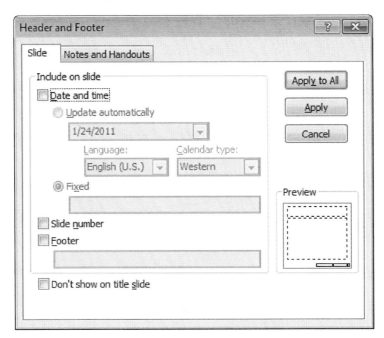

3.   From the **Slide** tab, select the **Date and time** option.

4.   Click the **Update automatically** option.

5.   Change the **Language** to **English (UK)**.

6.   Click the arrow in the date drop-down box to display a list of date formats. Select the third date option, e.g. **12 November, 2010**.

7.   Check the **Slide number** option to show slide numbers on all the slides.

8.   Check the **Footer** option, and then type **Designed by** in the **Footer** box and add your name afterwards.

> **Note:** *Notice the **Preview** image on the right which shows the options that are selected and where they will appear on the slides.*

Exercise 12 - Continued

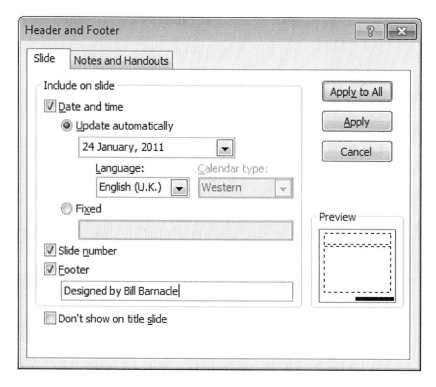

9. Click **Apply to All** to insert the information on to the slides.

10. View the **Slide Master** and look at the bottom of the slide.

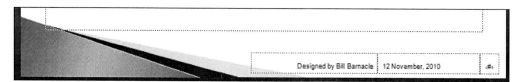

11. This shows the default position for the three footer text boxes in this theme. It is possible to click in any box and change the format or alignment of the content, or even to move any box to a different location by clicking and dragging.

> *Note:* *The colour of the footer text can be changed independently in **Slide Master** rather than editing theme colours.*

12. Close the **Master View** <u>without</u> changing anything.

13. Save the changes to the presentation.

14. Leave the presentation open for the next exercise.

Exercise 13 - Applying a Background

Knowledge:

Previous exercises have shown a slide background being added as part of a theme, but it is possible to add various background effects manually to slides. A background can be a plain solid colour, a colour gradient, a texture, a pattern or a picture.

Backgrounds can be applied to all slides (by being applied to the **Slide Master**) or they can be applied to the current slide only.

Activity:

1. Make sure the **themed** presentation is displayed, and then select the **Design** tab. From the **Background** group, click the **Background Styles** button.

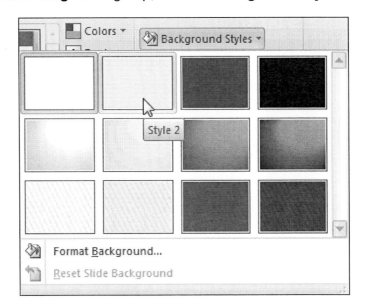

2. Roll the cursor over the options to see a preview on the slide. Select **Style 2** to apply it. Notice the background is applied to all the slides.

3. Click the **Background Styles** button again and select **Format Background** to display the **Format Background** dialog box.

4. Under **Fill**, select the **Picture or texture fill** option. Click the **Texture** drop-down.

5. Place the cursor over each background texture to display the name of that texture (in a **ToolTip**).

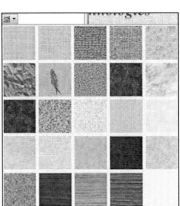

6. Select **Green marble**.

7. Click the **Apply to All** button, then click **Close**. The **Green Marble** background is applied to all the slides.

Exercise 13 - Continued

8. The new background was a poor choice. For example, the dark text on a dark background is not very easy to read.

9. Display the **Format Background** dialog box again and select **Gradient fill**.

10. Colour gradients can be selected from an existing list. Click **Preset Colors** and select **Moss** from the options. From **Type** select **Shade from title**. This affects how the graded colour will appear.

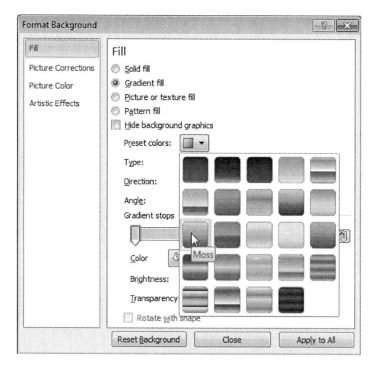

11. Click **Apply to All** to see the effect. Click **Close**. Notice how the title slide has colour graded differently from the others.

> **Note:** *Backgrounds can also be changed for individual slides.*

12. Select the first slide then display the **Format Background** dialog box again, and then select the **Picture or texture fill** option.

13. Any picture stored on your computer can be used as a background. Click **File** and locate the supplied data folder. Select the **cold** image file, then click **Insert**.

14. This time click **Close** to change the background of the selected slide only.

> **Note:** **Apply to All** *applies the background to all slides.*

15. Select the option to **Hide Background Graphics** from the **Background** group on the **Design** tab. This places the inserted picture in front.

16. Save the presentation and then close it.

Exercise 14 - Develop Your Skills

You will find a *Develop Your Skills* exercise at the end of each Skill Set. Work through it to ensure you've understood the previous exercises.

1. Open the presentation **Fashion**.

2. Apply the **Flow** theme.

3. Edit the **Color Scheme** so that **Accent1** is bright green.

4. Save the amended theme as **exercise14**.

5. Set up a **Slide Master** slide using the following house style as a guide:

NAME	FONT	POINT SIZE	FEATURE	ALIGNMENT
Title	Forte	60 pt	Standard (not bold)	Centre
Main Bullet	Garamond	40 pt	Italic with bullet character, e.g. ●	Left
Level 2 bullet	Brush Script MT	32 pt	No bullet point	Left

Note: *If the exact fonts listed above are not available, choose alternatives.*

FEATURE	POSITION
Slide Number	Bottom left
Your Name	Bottom centre
Date (Automatic)	Bottom right

Hint: *Slide numbers are already included on the right of the slides. You will need to remove these first.*

6. Add the image **woods.jpg**, which is supplied with the data for this unit, as a background to the title slide <u>only</u>.

7. Make sure the theme's background graphic is hidden.

8. Save the presentation as **fashion2** and close it.

Note: *Example solutions are given in the **Answers** section at the end of the guide.*

Summary: Presentation Styles

In this Skill Set you have started the presentation software program *PowerPoint*. You have opened, saved and closed presentations.

Your OCR ITQ evidence must demonstrate your ability to:

- Format complex presentations by:
  - Using themes
  - Applying backgrounds
  - Changing colour schemes

- Use the Slide Master to:
  - Define bullet levels
  - Add automatic fields

Skill Set 3

Templates

By the end of this Skill Set you should be able to:

Use an Existing Template
Create a New Template
Modify a Template
Use a Created Template
Apply a Saved Theme

Exercise 15 - Using an Existing Template

Knowledge:

Templates are previously designed *PowerPoint* presentations which can be used as a basis for new presentations. *PowerPoint* has a number of preinstalled templates, although new ones can be created easily. Companies may even have their own "in house" templates which contain corporate logos and fonts, and can be used as a starting point for business presentations.

Whether a new presentation is to be created from a template or from scratch, you should ensure that it is suitable for the target audience (for example, ask yourself if the fonts are large enough to read, are the colours confusing, etc.)?

Activity:

1.   From the **File** tab, select **New**.

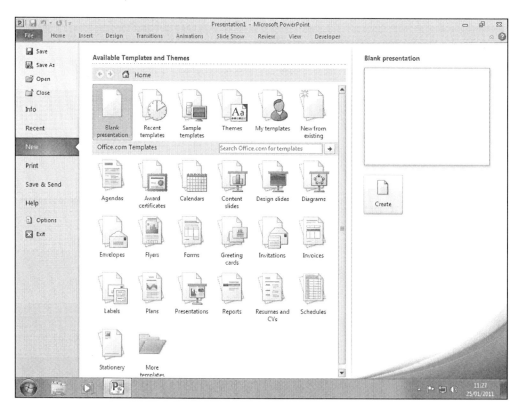

2.   All new presentations are started form here, including those started from a **template**.

3.   Under **Available Templates and Themes**, click on **Sample templates**.

4.   These are templates that are supplied with the program, although many more are available online.

5.   In **Sample templates**, **Classic Photo Album** is selected by default. A preview is shown on the right.

6.   Click on other templates to view the previews. Finally select **Quiz Show**.

Exercise 15 - Continued

7.   To start a new presentation based on this template, click **Create**. The presentation opens with the first slide displayed in the centre.

8.   Notice in the **Status Bar** that there are **8** slides and that the **Title Bar** shows **Presentation#** (where # is a number) rather than the name of the template.

9.   Click on each slide in turn to view the variety of text and graphics that have been included.

10.   There are more slides than can be displayed in the **Slides** area. Use the scroll bar to view the remainder.

11.   Click on **Outline** to view the text included in each slide. Return to **Slides**.

12.   Click back on slide **1**. Use the **Slide Show** button at the right of the **Status Bar** to run the slide show.

13.   This show does not run automatically. To display the answers of questions and to move from slide to slide, press the left mouse button. Various quiz question techniques are used in this presentation.

14.   At the end of the show, click to return to slide **1**.

> *Note:*   *Templates are used as a basis for other presentations, so it is expected that this presentation will be changed to add new questions and answers. Slides could be added and others removed.*

15.   Click once on the slide where **Quiz Show** is displayed. You can now edit this text (it is shown within a **Text Box** - notice the dotted square that appears).

16.   Change the title from **Quiz Show** to **ITQ Quiz**.

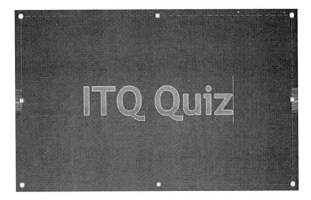

17.   Whether changes are made or not, to use this presentation again it must be saved with a new name. Click the **File** tab and select **Save As**.

18.   Make sure the file is being saved to the supplied data location. Change the name of the file to **quiz** and click **Save**.

19.   Close the presentation without making any further changes.

Exercise 16 - Creating a Template

Knowledge:

Having spent considerable time and effort designing a suitable appearance for your presentation, you may wish to apply the same look to subsequent slide shows that you create. Fortunately, any layout you create can be saved as a template and then used as a basis for further presentations so that all formatting styles and effects will be consistent. This is particularly relevant for organisations who may apply a house style to their presentations.

Activity:

1. To create a template, use the **Blank presentation** option from the **File** tab to create a new blank presentation.

2. Select the **Design** tab and apply the **Solstice** theme.

3. View the **Slide Master**. Click the uppermost slide on the left so that the main slide master is displayed.

4. Select the text **Click to edit Master title style** and select the **Home** tab.

5. Change the font to **Stencil** and the colour to red (from **Standard Colors**). Leave all other settings the same.

6. On the **Slide Master** tab, click **Background Styles**, | Background Styles ▾ |, and then select **Style 6**.

7. Click **Close Master View**.

> **Note:** You have now created a basic design that could be used as a starting point for future presentations.

8. The presentation now needs to be saved as a template so that it can be used over again. Click the **File** tab and select **Save As**.

9. In the **Save As** dialog box, change the **File name** to **adventure** and select **PowerPoint Template (*.potx)** from **Save as type**.

> **Note:** When this file type is selected, the save location will automatically jump to the **Templates** folder; the location of existing PowerPoint templates.

10. Click the **Save** button, | Save |.

> **Note:** Templates could be stored in any location but would not then be automatically available within the **My Templates** section of the **New Presentation** dialog box.

11. Close the template.

Exercise 17 - Amending a Template

Knowledge:

Like any presentation, a template can be opened, amended and saved. Any existing presentations which have been created based on that template will not be affected if the template changes later.

Activity:

1.   Click the **File** tab and select **New**. From **Available Templates and Themes**, click the **My templates** icon.

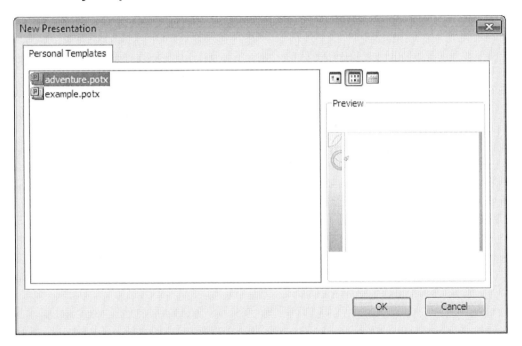

2.   Select the **adventure** template and click **OK**. A new presentation opens based on the template.

3.   View the **Slide Master** and select the main slide master from the top of the list.

4.   Select the first level bullet text (**Click to edit Master text styles**) and change the font to **Italic** and the colour to dark blue using the buttons on the **Home** tab.

Exercise 17 - Continued

5. Select the second level bullet text and similarly change the font to **Italic** and the colour to dark blue.

6. Display the **Slide Master** tab and then click **Close Master View**.

7. Click the **File** tab, and then select **Save As**.

8. In the **Save As** dialog box, select the **Save as type** to be a **PowerPoint Template** as before.

9. Change the **File name** to **adventure** and click **Save**.

10. To save the amended template, click **Yes**.

11. Close the updated template.

Exercise 18 - Using a Created Template

Knowledge:

Saved templates can be used in two main ways. They can be used as the basis for a new presentation, or they can be applied to existing presentations as **Design Templates**.

Activity:

1. Click the **File** tab and select **New**. Select **My templates**.

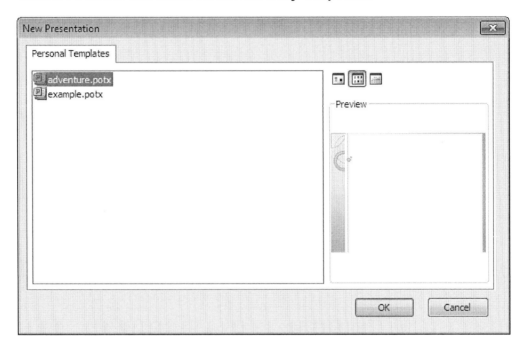

2. Select the **adventure** template from the list and click **OK**.

3. A new presentation is opened with no content but with the master slides defined with the required styles. A title slide is displayed.

4. Click in the **Title** area for the new slide and type **Adventure International**.

5. Click in the **Subtitle** area and type **Staff Presentation**.

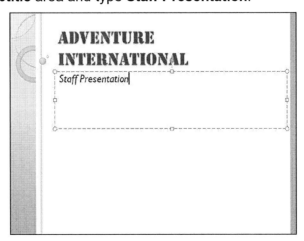

Exercise 18 - Continued

6. Display the **Home** tab, and then click the **New Slide** drop-down arrow.

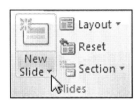

7. Select the **Title and Content** layout. A new slide is added.

> **Note:** *Notice that the new slide automatically adopts the template's styles.*

8. Save the new presentation as **adventure international** in the supplied data folder.

> **Note:** *After working with templates, PowerPoint sets the save location as the **Templates** folder (good for finding templates but not for storing ordinary presentations).*

9. To copy the formatting and styles of this template to other existing presentations, a new **Theme** can be created and then applied.

10. Display the **Design** tab and click the **More** button in the **Themes** group.

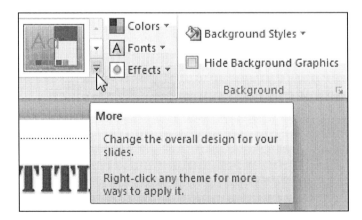

11. Click **Save Current Theme**.

> **Note:** *Notice that the save location is now a subfolder within the **Templates** folder.*

12. Enter the **File name** as **advent** (the extension **.thmx** is added automatically).

13. Click **Save** to save this theme.

> **Note:** *The theme is now available to other presentations, which you will see in the next exercise.*

14. Close the presentation <u>without</u> saving.

Exercise 19 - Applying a Saved Theme

Knowledge:

After creating a template containing custom styles and saving it as a new **Theme**, it can then be applied to other created presentations so that they conform.

Activity:

1.   Open the presentation **Holiday**. This is a presentation already created for the *Adventure International Company*, but it does not use the correct style.

2.   Select the **Design** tab. Click the **More** arrow, 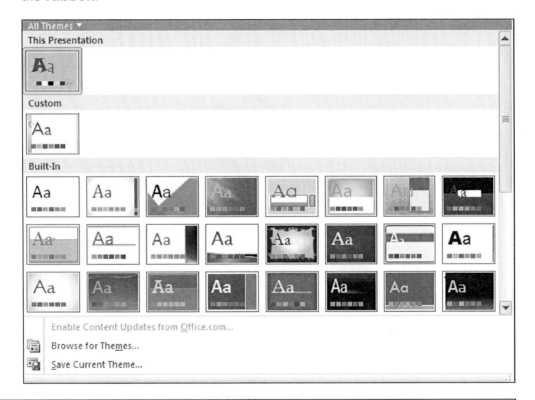, at the right of **Themes** on the **Ribbon**.

> **Note:**   At the top of **All Themes** is the theme of the current presentation. Beneath it, under **Custom**, is the **Advent** theme saved in the last exercise.

3.   Place the cursor on the **advent** theme to show the **ToolTip**.

4.   Click on the **advent** theme to apply it. Notice that all the content from the original presentation has been retained – even the bear logo in the lower right of every slide – but the styles have all been updated.

> **Note:**   If the bear logo is always required as part of the house style, it should be included on the master slide of the **Adventure** template.

5.   Save the presentation as **holiday1** and close it.

Exercise 20 - Develop Your Skills

You will find a *Develop Your Skills* exercise at the end of each Skill Set. Work through it to ensure you've understood the previous exercises.

1. Start a new, blank presentation.

2. Open **Slide Master** and select the main **Slide Master** (the one at the top of the slide master pane).

3. Apply a **Theme** of **Origin**.

4. Centre the middle **Footer** text box and right align the date (hint: select the text box rather than the text inside).

5. Insert a **Footer**. Include on the slide: the date to update automatically, a slide number, and a footer containing your name.

6. Apply these changes to **all** slides. Check on the other slide masters that your name is centred and the date appears on the right.

7. Apply a background to **all** master slides using the texture effect **Stationery**.

8. On the **Slide Master**, change the font size for the **Master title style** to **40 pt**.

9. On the **Slide Master**, change the **Master text style** (1ˢᵗ level bullets) to **Bold**, **Italic**, and a line spacing of **1.5** lines.

10. Change the second level bullet font size to **20 pt**.

11. **Close Master View** and save the presentation as a template (in the default *PowerPoint* **Templates** folder) with a name of **collegetemp**.

12. Save the theme as **college** and then close the template.

13. Start a new presentation based on the **collegetemp** template.

14. On the title slide, add a title of **Toffington College**, and add a subtitle of **Passing on Knowledge**.

15. Apply the **Apex** theme. Notice the changes. Then apply the **college** theme saved earlier.

16. Save the presentation in the folder with the supplied data files with a name of **develop3**.

17. Close the presentation.

> **Note:**   *Example solutions are given in the **Answers** section at the end of the guide.*

Summary: Templates

The skills in this Skill Set are concerned with how to make use of templates when developing presentations. You have created presentations using existing templates, created new templates, modified templates and applied saved themes.

Your ITQ evidence must demonstrate the following skills:

- Using existing templates, including:
    - Designs and styles
    - Organisational guidelines

- Adapting and creating new templates

- Choosing, using and adjusting templates for presentations

Skill Set 4

Editing Content

By the end of this Skill Set you should be able to:

Use Undo and Redo
Use Cut, Copy and Paste
Use the Drag and Drop Technique
Understand Copyright Issues
Import Text
Insert Text
Find and Replace Data

Exercise 21 - Using Undo and Redo

Knowledge:

Undo and Redo are very useful features, which help correct errors. Undo allows the reversal of incorrect actions, while Redo repeats the undone action. It is also possible to undo/redo multiple actions at the same time.

Activity:

1. Open the **Course** presentation.

2. Click on slide **3**, **Skill Check Matrix**, to select it, and switch to **Normal** view (if not already selected).

3. Highlight all of the text on the first, second level bullet, **1 - no knowledge of the subject** and press **<Delete>**.

4. Move the mouse over the **Undo** button on the **Quick Access Toolbar**. The first menu choice will say **Undo Clear**. Click on it and the deleted text will be displayed again.

5. Move the mouse over the **Redo** button. The **ToolTip** should say **Redo Clear**. Click on it and the text will be deleted again.

6. Click on the drop-down arrow of the **Undo** button, ![undo drop-down]. A list of recent actions that can be undone will appear.

> **Note:** When there are no actions that can be undone, the **Undo** button will be unavailable. When there are many actions that can be undone, the scroll bar may have to be used to view all of the listed items.

7. Click on the top action to undo it.

8. Click **Redo**, ![redo button], to redo the last action. The text will be deleted again.

9. Click **Undo** one last time to replace the text.

10. Leave the presentation open for the next exercise.

Exercise 22 - Using Copy and Paste

Knowledge:

The **Copy** and **Paste** commands allow text and other items (such as graphics) to be copied and used in different parts of a presentation. It is often quicker to copy an object and then amend it than to recreate it. When an item is copied, it remains in its original location.

Copied text is placed in a temporary storage area known as the **Clipboard**. Up to **24** copied items can be held on the **Clipboard**, which is common to all *Windows* applications and can be displayed in the **Clipboard** task pane.

Copy and **Paste** can also be used to obtain content from other presentations or from other applications, such as word processed documents or spreadsheets. This is covered in later exercises.

Activity:

1. Using the **Course** presentation, select the **Home** tab and click the **Clipboard** launcher, to display the **Clipboard** task pane.

2. If there are any entries, click **Clear All**, , in the task pane to remove them.

3. Display slide **7**, and then select the text **By phone on 0191 549 5002**.

> **Note:** To select an entire bullet point's text, simply click the bullet symbol.

4. Click the **Copy** button, . The icon for the copied text is placed on the **Clipboard**, but the original text remains in place.

Exercise 22 - Continued

5. On the slide, place the insertion before the line **E-mail us on...**

6. On the **Clipboard**, click the copied icon. The **By phone...** line is pasted below the original.

> **Note:** The default, when clicking the **Paste** button, the last item copied is pasted. Using the **Clipboard** allows more complex copy and paste operations to be performed.

7. At this point any items copied will still be displayed on the **Clipboard**. Any of them can be pasted again as many times as required.

> **Note:** Sometimes a **Paste Smart Tag**, [📋 (Ctrl) ▾], is displayed next to pasted text. Clicking on the tag displays formatting options; either to keep the formatting the text had at source, or to let it take on the format of its new location.

8. Select the word **phone** (with no extra space) on the copied line.

> ➢By phone on 0191 549 5002
> ➢By **phone** on 0191 549 5002

9. Type in **fax**.

10. In the same way, change the number to the fax number **549 9005**.

> ➢By phone on 0191 549 5002
> ➢By fax on 0191 549 9005

11. Save the presentation as **course3**.

12. Leave the presentation and the **Clipboard** task pane open for the next exercise.

Exercise 23 - Using Cut and Paste

Knowledge:

The **Cut** and **Paste** commands allow text and other items, such as graphics, to be moved around a presentation from one place to another quickly and easily. It is much quicker to cut and paste text, for example, than to delete and then retype it somewhere else. When an item is cut, it is <u>removed</u> from its original location.

Activity:

1. With the **course3** presentation still open in **Normal** view, view slide **6**, **Summary**.

2. The last bullet point is on the wrong slide. Highlight the whole bullet point.

3. Click the **Cut** button, , on the **Clipboard** group. The text is removed from the slide and an entry appears on the **Clipboard**.

4. View slide **2**, **Introduction**, place the insertion point at the end of the second bullet line, after the word **course**.

5. Press <**Enter**> to create a new empty bullet line.

6. Either click the entry on the **Clipboard** or click **Paste**. The cut text is pasted as the new bullet point (delete any extra bullets that may appear).

7. Notice that at this point all of the items cut or copied during these exercises are still displayed on the **Clipboard**. Any of them can be pasted again as many times as required.

8. As an alternative to copy and paste, **drag** and **drop** can be used. Select slide **5**. Move the cursor over the last bullet until it changes to a white four-headed cross.

9. Click to select the bullet and its attached text. Place the cursor over the selection and hold down the mouse button. The cursor changes to a white arrow with a box below.

10. **Drag** the selection up the slide. A feint line indicates where the bullet will be placed. Drag it above the first bullet and **drop** it, i.e. release the mouse button.

11. Save and close the presentation. Click **Clear All**, , to clear the **Clipboard** but leave the task pane open.

Exercise 24 - Importing Text

Knowledge:

Copy and **Paste** can be used to import text or other objects into a *PowerPoint* presentation from another source.

However, when using any content that is copied or imported from a different source, you need to be aware of **copyright**. The effect of copyright on the day to day use of IT is that any text, picture, audio or video file – whether scanned in, downloaded or copied from the Internet, or from any other source – <u>cannot</u> be used in a presentation unless permission is given by its author. Content may be used if the owner has given explicit consent, but in this case it is customary to include a reference to acknowledge the source of the material.

Entering text which is a copy of someone else's work or ideas, and passing it off as your own, is plagiarism. Whilst this is not necessarily illegal, it is usually considered as immoral. If you are quoting from someone's work, a reference must be given.

Activity:

1. Open the presentation **Far North3**.

2. Insert a new **Title and Content** slide after slide **3**, and make sure the **Clipboard** task pane is displayed.

3. Open *Microsoft Word*, click the **File** tab and select **Open**. In the **Open** dialog box, navigate to the supplied data files and make sure **Files of type** is set to **All Files**.

4. Open the text file **products.txt**. All the text needed for a new slide is contained in this file. Text in capitals is not to be used.

5. If the **Clipboard** is not displayed, click the **Clipboard** launcher (this is the same in *Word* as it is in *PowerPoint*).

6. Copy the **Title** text indicated for slide **4**, i.e. **Product Divisions**.

7. Copy the six bullet lines as one block.

8. Switch back to *PowerPoint*. Click in the slide **4** heading area and click the new title text on the **Clipboard** (remove any unnecessary new lines).

Exercise 24 - Continued

9.   Click in the slide **4** bullet area and click the bullet text on the **Clipboard**.

10. Use the **Increase List Level** feature from the **Paragraph** group to demote points **2**, **4** and **6** to second level.

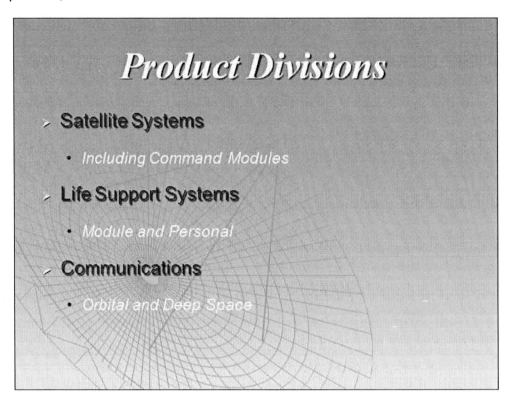

11. Close the **Clipboard**.

12. Save the presentation as **imported** and leave it open.

13. In *Word*, close the text file <u>without</u> saving.

14. Leave the *Word* application open for the next exercise.

Exercise 25 - Inserting Text

Knowledge:

Text can be inserted into *PowerPoint* directly without using copy and paste. The insert process can be used with documents formatted with correct bullet levels, or with existing slides from other presentations. Inserting other objects such as pictures and tables is covered in the next Skill Set.

Activity:

1. Using *Microsoft Word*, open the file **Conditions.docx**, which is included with the supplied data files. Make sure **Outline** view is selected.

2. Examine the text; it has been formatted at different levels.

> **Note:** When imported into PowerPoint, the highest level will be translated into slide titles, the next level into 1st level bullet points, and so on.

3. Close the document and close the word processing application.

4. In *PowerPoint*, the **imported** presentation should be open. Select slide **4**, **Product Divisions**, and click the drop-down arrow on the **New Slide** button.

5. Select **Slides from Outline**.

6. Make sure the location of the supplied data files is shown and **Files of type** is set to **All Outlines**.

7. Select the file **Conditions** and click the **Insert** button, | Insert |▼|.

8. Two new slides are created from the outline file. Look at them in **Normal** view and compare their structure with the original file layout.

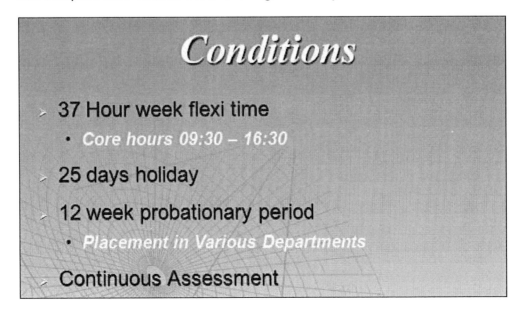

Exercise 25 - Continued

9. Content can also be inserted from other presentations. View slide **6**, **Benefits**, and click the drop-down arrow on the **New Slide** button. Select **Reuse Slides**.

10. In the pane at the right, click the **Browse** button and select **Browse File**. Select the location of the supplied data files.

11. Select the presentation **Old** from the list and click **Open**.

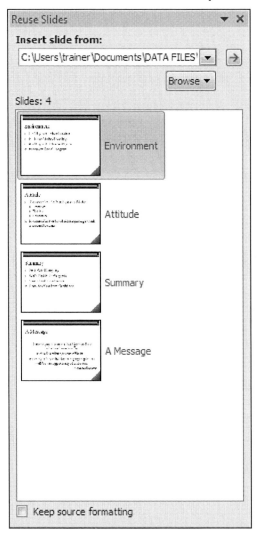

12. Move the mouse pointer over each slide to view the content. Click on each one in turn to insert it.

> **Note:** *There is an option in the pane to keep the original source formatting for the inserted slides. Do <u>not</u> select it in this exercise.*

13. Close the **Reuse Slides** pane.

14. All four slides are inserted into the presentation. There may be a delay as the slides are reformatted to match the design. View each in turn.

15. Save the presentation, using the same file name **imported**, and close it.

Exercise 26 - Find and Replace Data

Knowledge:

Rather than finding and editing text manually, *PowerPoint* – like many other applications – has a replace option, making the process much quicker. This allows specified text to be replaced. **Replace** has an option to find and replace each occurrence individually or to **Replace All** occurrences.

Activity:

1.   Open the **Holiday** presentation. The word **dangerous** has been used in the presentation, which does not convey the right message to potential clients.

2.   On the **Home** tab, click ⌐ab̦ᵃᶜ Replace ▾⌐.

3.   In the **Find what** box, enter **dangerous**. In the **Replace with** box enter **exciting**.

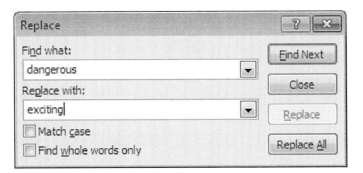

4.   Select **Find Next**. The first occurrence of the word **dangerous** is highlighted.

> **Note:**   *Selecting **Replace All** will automatically replace all occurrences of the word without indicating where they are.*

5.   Choose to **Replace** this occurrence. If there is another occurrence of the word, it will be highlighted.

6.   Select **Replace** to replace the next occurrence within the presentation. When there are no more occurrences of the word, a prompt will appear.

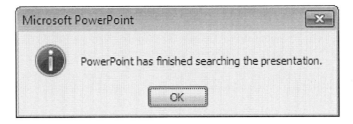

7.   At the prompt click **OK**, then close the **Replace** dialog box.

8.   Save the presentation as **holiday2** and close it.

Exercise 27 - Develop Your Skills

You will find a *Develop Your Skills* exercise at the end of each Skill Set. Work through it to ensure you've understood the previous exercises.

1. Open the presentation **develop3**, created earlier. If you have not created **develop3** open the supplied presentation **College3** and save it as **develop3**.

2. Create a new **Title and Content** slide after the title slide.

3. Open the text file **intro1**. Use copy and paste to import the text from the file onto the new slide **2** of the presentation. The first line is the slide title, the remaining four lines are bullet points.

4. Close the text file.

5. On slide **2** of the presentation, use cut and paste to reverse the order of the bullet points so that the first bullet point becomes the last, etc. Make sure there are no blank bullet points left on the slide.

6. Open the document **intro2**. This has been formatted with outline heading styles so that it can be directly inserted into a presentation. Close the document.

7. From the **New Slide** drop-down, select **Slides from Outline** to create a new slide **3** in the presentation, based on the **intro2** document.

8. Insert all the slides from the **Subjects** presentation into the **develop3** presentation so that they become slides **4 - 9**.

9. The content of slides **8** and **9** are in the wrong order. Use copy and paste techniques to reverse the content of these slides (don't simply use **Slide Sorter** view to move them).

10. Use the **Replace** function to change all occurrences of the word **subjects** to the word **courses**.

11. Capitalise the word **courses** found in any of the titles.

12. Add footers to all the imported slides.

13. Check the footer alignment for each of the individual slides.

14. Save the presentation as **develop4** and close it.

Note:	Example solutions are given in the **Answers** section at the end of the guide.

Summary: Editing Content

The skills in this Skill Set are concerned with how to add and amend text content in your presentation. You have used undo, redo, cut, copy, paste and drag and drop. You have also inserted text, imported text and used find and replace.

Attention has been drawn to copyright issues when using information from sources other than your own.

Your ITQ evidence must demonstrate the following skills:

- An understanding of copyright law (e.g. on music downloads or use of other peoples' images), acknowledgement of sources, avoiding plagiarism, equal opportunities, local guidelines

- Inserting text and slides from other presentations

- Importing information produced using other software

- Editing slide content using:
    - Undo and redo
    - Cut, copy and paste
    - Drag and drop

Skill Set 5

PowerPoint Objects

By the end of this Skill Set you should be able to:

Insert and Format Diagrams
Insert Clip Art and Pictures from File
Move and Resize Objects
Delete Objects
Insert Objects on Master Slides
Crop Pictures
Align Data using Tabs
Use Tables
Insert and Format a Chart

Exercise 28 - Inserting a Diagram

Knowledge:

Slides in a presentation are composed of various objects which can result in an impressive show. When creating a company presentation, it can be useful to insert a diagram such a flowchart, an organisation chart etc.

Activity:

1. Start a new, blank presentation.

2. Change the layout to **Title and Content** and add the slide title **Flowchart**.

3. From the icons in the centre of the slide, click **Insert SmartArt Graphic**.

4. The **Choose a SmartArt Graphic** dialog box appears.

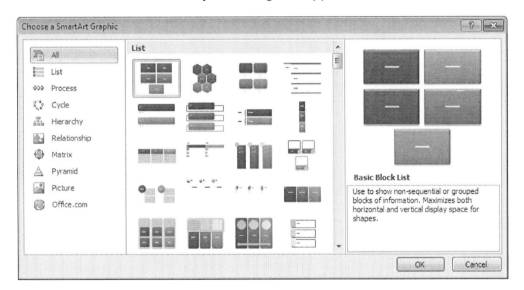

5. Look at the diagrams available, clicking on each type in turn from the list on the left to see a list of graphics in that category on the right.

6. Select **Process** from the left and then **Basic Process** on the right (top left icon). This is a flowchart.

7. Click **OK** to insert the diagram on the slide.

8. In the first text box on the diagram, enter **Alarm rings**. In the next box enter, **Get out of bed**, and in the third **Get dressed**.

9. With the third box selected, display the **SmartArt Tools Design** tab, click the **Add Shape** button's drop-down, and select **Add Shape After** to add another **Process** box.

10. Enter the text **Go to work**.

Exercise 28 - Continued

11. The type of box can be changed. Select the second box and display the **Format** tab. Click the **Change Shape** button to display the variety of shapes.

> **Note:** *Shapes can be added to any slide in any position using the **Shapes** button in the **Illustrations** group on the **Insert** tab.*

12. Locate the **Flowchart** section and select **Flowchart: Decision**, ◇.

13. Select the last box and change the shape to **Flowchart: Terminator**, ⬭.

14. Use a centre handle to reduce the height of the selected box by half.

15. Display the **SmartArt Tools' Design** tab.

16. Click the **More** button of the **SmartArt Styles** and select **Brick Scene**.

17. The style of the diagram changes to reflect the selection.

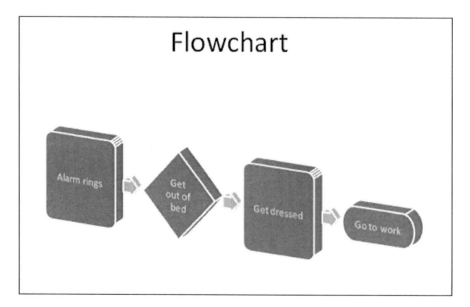

18. Save the presentation as **flowchart**.

19. Experiment with the box types, styles and text effects.

20. Close the presentation <u>without</u> saving.

Exercise 29 - Organisation Charts

Knowledge:

When creating a company presentation, it can be useful to insert an organisation chart to demonstrate the company's structure. A slide containing a chart can easily be created.

Activity:

1. Open the **Far North4** presentation and display slide **3**, **Far North Technologies**, in **Normal** view.

2. Click the drop-down arrow on the **New Slide** button. Select the **Title and Content** layout.

3. Add the slide title **Structure**.

4. Click **Insert SmartArt Graphic**, [icon]. Select **Hierarchy** from the left, and then select **Organization Chart** (top left) and click **OK**.

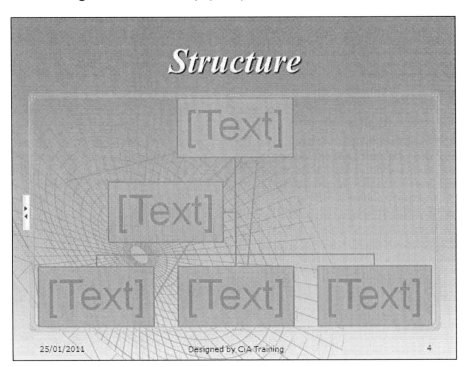

Note:	If the **Type your text here** box is displayed, close it. This can be used as an alternative to entering text on the slide.

5. Click in the top box, and type **Conrad North**. Press <**Enter**> and then type **Director**.

Note:	The boxes are automatically resized and moved as the chart is created.

6. Click on the border of the box directly below **Conrad North**. This box is not needed; press <**Delete**> to remove it.

Exercise 29 - Continued

7.   Click in the leftmost of the three boxes and enter **David Oram** on the first line and **Products** on the second line.

8.   Click in the middle of the three boxes and enter **Linda Choi**, **Operations**.

9.   Delete the third box.

10. David Oram has three product managers reporting to him; click on the box for **David Oram**, then click the **Add Shape** drop-down button to show a list of shapes positions available.

11. Select **Add Shape Below** to create a box linked to David's. Click in the new box and enter **Tom Malone, Satellite Systems**. David is Tom's boss.

12. Add two more subordinates to David Oram; **Katharine Deacon**, **Life Support** and **Sahab Khan**, **Communications**. Remember to select the box for David before adding each new shape.

13. Add two subordinates to Linda Choi; **Susan Clarke**, **Sales** and **Paul Costa**, **Administration**.

14. Linda Choi has an assistant named **John Lightfoot**, **Audits**. Use **Add Assistant** from the **Add Shape** options to create and complete the box.

15. Click on the slide away from the chart to see how it will appear. It should have a similar layout to that shown below.

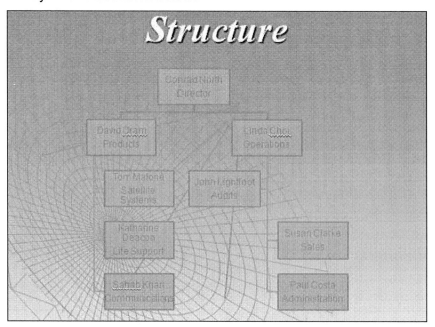

16. Click on **David Oram**. From **Layout** in the **Create Graphic** group, select **Standard**. Repeat for **Linda Choi**.

17. Save the presentation as **objects** and leave it open.

Exercise 30 - Formatting Organisation Charts

Knowledge:

Organisation charts can be formatted to change colours, fonts, etc.

Activity:

1. With the presentation **objects** still open from the previous exercise, view slide **4**, the organisation chart.

2. Click on the chart (not in a box) to select it. The chart will be enclosed by a grey border, , when selected.

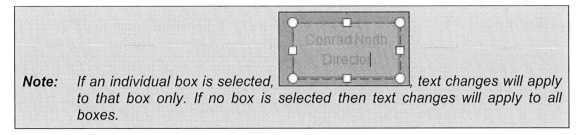

> **Note:** *If an individual box is selected, text changes will apply to that box only. If no box is selected then text changes will apply to all boxes.*

3. Ensure that no individual boxes are selected and then display the **Home** tab.

4. From the **Font** area, select the **Tahoma** font, the **Bold** font style, and a font **Size** of **12**. Select a dark blue for the **Font Color**.

> **Note:** *To select several boxes, drag a rectangle on the slide, which completely encloses all the required boxes. Check that all the required boxes have handles to indicate they are selected.*

5. With the chart still selected, select the **Format** tab from **SmartArt Tools**.

6. Click **Shape Effects**, ⬜ Shape Effects ▾, select **Bevel**, and then click **Circle**.

> **Note:** *Options from the **Design** tab of **SmartArt Tools** can also be used to change the appearance of the organisation chart.*

7. Save the presentation and leave it open.

Exercise 31 - Inserting Clip Art

Knowledge:

Clip Art is a vast store of pictures, available within all *Microsoft Office* products.

Clip Art can be added to individual slides or to the **Slide Master**, in which case it will appear on all slides. The **Clip Art** task pane contains tools to search the available graphics using keywords, so that appropriate clips can be found quickly.

Note: *Many of the large number of graphics included with Office 2010 are stored online. If graphics used in the following exercises are unavailable, replace the specified graphic with an alternative.*

Activity:

1. Display slide **2**, **A Fresh Career**, in the **objects** presentation.

2. Select the **Insert** tab and click **Clip Art**. The **Clip Art** task pane appears.

3. **Clip Art** content can be searched for. Type **rocket** in the **Search for** box.

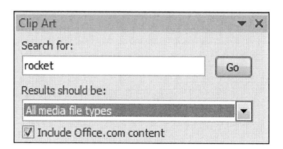

4. The **Results should be** box should read **All media type files** so that all possible sources of graphics are searched. To see what kind of files will be included in the search, click the drop-down arrow on the **Results should be** box.

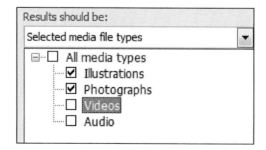

5. In the example shown, clip art and photograph files will be searched, but not movies or sounds. For this exercise make sure **All media types** is selected. Options can be selected to narrow down the search.

Exercise 31 - Continued

6. Click the **Go** button, Go , and, after a short delay, a list of **Clip Art** images for this subject will be displayed in the task pane.

7. Use the scroll bar at the right to browse through the available images, then locate a suitable picture from the list.

8. Click on the required image to insert it on to the slide.

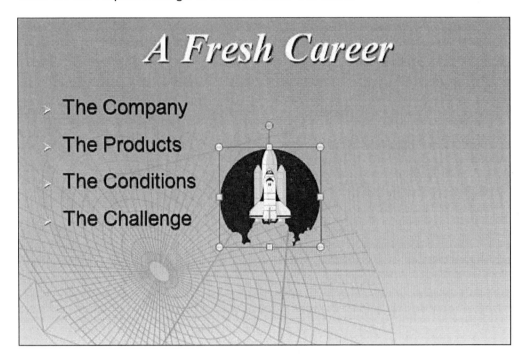

9. Close the **Clip Art** task pane.

10. Save the presentation and leave it open.

Exercise 32 - Moving and Resizing Objects

Knowledge:

When an object such as a chart or picture is added to a slide, it may not be in the correct position or of the required size. It can be moved and/or resized to suit.

Activity:

1.   Slide **2** of the **objects** presentation should still be open in **Normal** view. The inserted image should have eight white handles to indicate that it is selected. If it does not, click once on the image and they will appear.

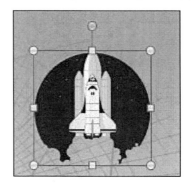

2.   To move the object, click in the middle of it – the cursor changes to a four way arrow, 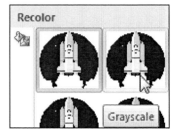.

3.   While holding down the mouse button, move it around the screen. The object will be positioned wherever the mouse button is released. Practise doing this, and then move the object to the right of the slide.

4.   The handles can be used to resize the picture. Move the cursor over the handles. When moving over a corner handle the cursor changes to a diagonal double headed arrow, e.g. .

5.   When one of these handles is clicked and dragged, it will resize the object *proportionally*. Click on the top left handle and drag up and left. The image is made larger, but remains in proportion. Make it roughly double the size.

> **Note:** *The handles in the centre of the object edges are used less often because they resize the object in one direction only and therefore distort the shape.*

6.   The colours may be too bright. Click on the **Picture Tools Format** tab, and then click the **Color** button. Select **Grayscale** from the **Recolor** gallery.

7.   Save the presentation and leave it open for the next exercise.

Exercise 33 - Object Orientation

Knowledge:

The orientation of inserted objects such as images can be altered in several different ways. Unwanted objects can easily be deleted.

Activity:

1. Slide **2** of the **objects** presentation should still be open in **Normal** view. Make sure the inserted image is selected.

2. Just above the top white handles of the image, a green circular handle is visible. When the cursor moves over this it becomes a circular arrow 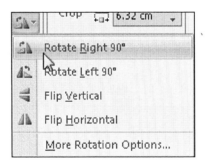.

3. Click and drag this handle from side to side to rotate the image.

4. Return it to its upright position.

5. From the **Arrange** group of the **Format** tab, click **Rotate**, . Select the **Rotate Right 90°** option. The image is turned 90 degrees clockwise.

6. Click **Rotate** again and select **Flip Horizontal**. The image is turned 180 degrees anti-clockwise.

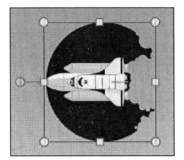

7. The management team have decided they do not like the graphic. Select it.

8. To delete it, press **<Delete>**. There is no warning message before the object is removed, but remember that the **Undo** command will reverse the deletion.

9. Leave the presentation open for the next exercise.

Exercise 34 - Objects on Slide Master

Knowledge:

When an object such as a **Clip Art** graphic or picture is added to the **Slide Master**, it can be moved and resized in the normal manner, but it will appear on every slide in the presentation.

Activity:

1. In the **objects** presentation, select the **View** tab and click **Slide Master**. Select the main slide master, not a layout slide.

2. Display the **Clip Art** task pane if not already on view.

3. Type **atoms** in the **Search for** box and click ⌐Go¬.

4. Select a suitable small image and click to insert it.

5. Resize the image to roughly **5cm** square (use the **Size** group to measure an object) and move it to the lower right corner of the slide.

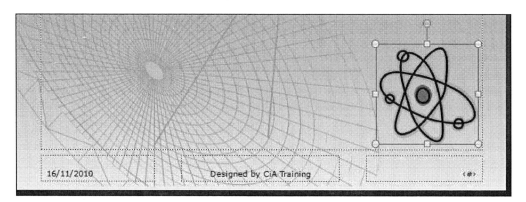

6. As this image will appear on every slide there is a chance it will obscure data. To avoid this, it can be made much less conspicuous. Select the image and click ⌐Color ▾¬.

7. Select **Washout** from the **Recolor** gallery.

8. Close the slide master to return to **Normal** view.

9. The image is now fainter and will always appear behind any other objects. Look through the slides to see the changes.

10. Close the **Clip Art** task pane.

11. Save the presentation and leave it open.

Exercise 35 - Inserting a Picture from File

Knowledge:

Any image file which is stored on your computer (or accessible from it) can be included on a slide. This includes downloaded library pictures (subject to copyright restrictions), photos downloaded from your digital camera or mobile phone, or files produced by graphic image programs such as *Adobe Photoshop* and *Paint Shop Pro* and saved in various formats, such as **.jpg**, **.gif**, **.bmp**, etc.

Activity:

1. In the **objects** presentation, insert a new **Picture with Caption** slide after the last slide. A **caption** is non bulleted text used to describe an object.

2. Add a title **Polaris** and the text **Company Mascot** (the caption).

3. Click the **Insert Picture from File** button from the **Insert** tab. The **Insert Picture** dialog box appears.

> **Note:** Alternatively, click on the icon in the centre of the slide.

4. Make sure the dialog box shows the location of the supplied data. Select the image file **polaris**. The photograph was loaded directly from a digital camera into the folder.

5. Click [Insert ▼]. The picture is inserted on the slide and fits the picture box.

6. With the picture still selected, display the **Picture Tools Format** tab. The **Adjust** group is used to manipulate the picture.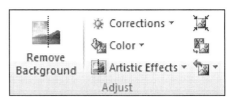

7. Click the **Corrections** drop-down in the **Adjust** group and select **Brightness +20% Contrast -40%**.

8. Experiment with the options in the **Adjust** group.

9. Click **Reset Picture** button 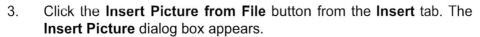 to return the picture to its original settings.

> **Note:** There are options to **Reset Picture** or **Reset Picture and Size** from within this button. The default setting is **Reset Picture**, occurring when the button is clicked without using the menu.

10. Save the presentation and leave it open.

Exercise 36 - Cropping a Picture

Knowledge:

Any images, including **Clip Art**, can be edited by cropping unwanted areas.

Activity:

1.　In the **objects** presentation, display slide **12**, **Polaris**, and select the mascot image.

2.　If the **Format** tab from **Picture Tools** is not visible, select it.

3.　Click the **Crop** button from the **Size** group. The handles around the image change.

4.　Click and drag any of these cropping handles inwards over the picture and then release the mouse button. The picture will now be cropped.

5.　Use different handles to crop the picture into the desired form. Try to end with a picture of just the face.

6.　Click away from the picture to remove the cropping handles. The new picture can be moved and resized like any other.

7.　With the image selected, click the **Reset Picture** drop-down arrow, 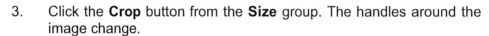, and select **Reset Picture & Size**. The picture is restored to its original form.

8.　Save the presentation and leave it open.

Exercise 37 - Aligning Data with Tabs

Knowledge:

There is often a need for data to appear on a slide in tabular form. The simplest way to do this is to use a list with tab settings.

Activity:

1. In the **objects** presentation, insert a new **Title and Content** slide after the last slide.

2. Add a title of **Department Staff** then click in the area **Click to add text**.

3. Press <**Ctrl Tab**>, type **Satellite**, press <**Tab**>, type **95**, press <**Enter**>.

> **Note:** <***Ctrl Tab***> *is needed to enter the first tab setting because **Tab** on its own would just demote the bullet to second level.*

4. Enter the following three lines:

    <**Ctrl Tab**>, **Life Support**, <**Tab**>, **81**, <**Enter**>.

    <**Ctrl Tab**>, **Communications**, <**Tab**>, **113**, <**Enter**>.

    <**Ctrl Tab**>, **Operations**, <**Tab**>, **67**, <**Enter**>.

5. Do not worry if the text does not appear to be lined up at this stage; this will happen when the tabs are set.

6. If the ruler is not displayed, select the **View** tab and check **Ruler**, ☑ Ruler .

7. Select all of the text in the list. Click the **Tab** button, ⌞, at the left of the ruler until the right tab, ⌟, is displayed.

8. Click once on the ruler at **10cm** to set the tab.

9. Click the **Tab** button, ⌟, at the left of the ruler until the decimal tab, ⌶, is displayed.

10. With all the text still selected, click once on the ruler at **14cm** to set the tab.

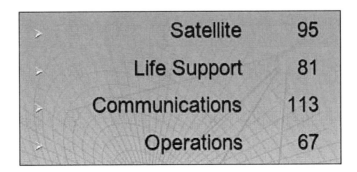

11. Save the presentation using the same file name and leave it open.

Exercise 38 - Tables

Knowledge:

Tables can be a useful tool for aligning data on slides. Tables can be created within *PowerPoint*, or they can be imported from another application such as *Excel*.

Activity:

1. In the **objects** presentation, insert a new slide after the last slide, with a layout of **Title and Content**.

2. Add a title of **Major Missions**.

3. Click on the **Insert Table** icon, in the centre of the slide, to display the **Insert Table** dialog box.

> **Note:** *Alternatively, click the **Table** button on the **Insert** tab and click and drag on any blank slide to create a table.*

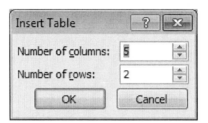

4. From the dialog box, select **3** columns by **4** rows and then click **OK**. A table appears on the slide. The **Table Tools** appear on the **Ribbon**.

5. Enter the data below into the table, using the <**Tab**> key to move from cell to cell.

Year	Mission	Destination
2003	Dark Side 2	Dark side of the Moon
2004	Thunderbird 4	Mars Orbiter
2005	Starburst	Galaxy Centre

6. Click the **Layout** tab from **Table Tools**. Click and drag to select the content in the table.

7. Click the **Center Vertically** button, from the **Alignment** group, to ensure all text is centred vertically in the table.

8. With the whole table still selected, select the **Design** tab. Click the **Text Effects** button, from **Word Styles** and select **Shadow**, then the first **Outer Shadow** style.

Exercise 38 - Continued

9.   Redisplay the **Layout** tab. Click and drag to select only the text on the top row. Make it centred (horizontally).

10.   Insert another new slide at the end of the presentation, with a layout of **Title Only**. Add a title of **Turnover**. The table for this slide will be copied from a spreadsheet.

11.   Start *Excel* and open the **Turnover** workbook, which will be found with the supplied data files.

12.   Click and drag to select the table (**A1:D5**). Click **Copy**, 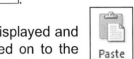.

13.   Switch back to *PowerPoint*, make sure the new slide is displayed and the title is <u>not</u> selected. Click **Paste**. The table is pasted on to the slide.

14.   The formatting of the table in *Excel* will also be copied from the spreadsheet and will usually not be appropriate for a presentation slide. Select the whole table and change the font to **24pt bold**.

15.   Click and drag the table borders to resize it until all the text is on a single line.

16.   Move the table to the centre of the slide.

17.   Select the numerical data only and centre it horizontally in the cells.

Turnover (million£)			
Division	2003	2004	2005
Satellite	5.1	4	5.8
Life Support	3	4.1	4.9
Communications	1.5	3.1	6.3

18.   Close *Excel* <u>without</u> saving any changes to the workbook.

19.   Save the presentation and leave it open

Exercise 39 - Inserting Charts

Knowledge:

A chart can be inserted on to a slide to display data in a more attractive way. The relevant information is entered into a datasheet and is then converted into a chart.

Activity:

1. In the **objects** presentation, insert a new slide after the last slide, with a layout of **Title and Content**.

2. Add a title of **Turnover 2** then click on the chart icon, ▊▊, to add a chart.

3. **Column** charts are already selected in the **Insert Chart** dialog box. Make sure the **Clustered Column** (first) subtype is selected and click **OK**.

> **Note:** A column chart is created in this exercise. When creating a pie chart, the positioning of data is important. The category must go along the top, not at the left, and the figures must be beneath it.

4. *Excel's* chart program starts and some preset data is displayed in a window at the right of the screen. Replace this data with the information from the table on the previous slide, as in the diagram below. Delete the data in row 5.

5. Drag the bottom right corner of the data range up to remove the extra row.

	A	B	C	D
1		2003	2004	2005
2	Satellite	5.1	4	5.8
3	Life Support	3	4.1	4.9
4	Communica	1.5	3.1	6.3
5				
6				

6. Close *Excel* by clicking the **File** tab and selecting **Close**.

7. Click on the slide, away from the chart, to remove the **Chart Tools** and see how the chart will appear on the slide.

8. Insert another **Title and Content** slide.

9. Enter the title **Total Sales** then click on the chart icon, ▊▊, to add a chart.

10. Select **Pie** from the list on the left and **Pie in 3-D** from the right.

11. Click **OK**.

Exercise 39 - Continued

12. Replace this data with **Sales**, as in the diagram below.

	A	B
1		Sales
2	Satellite	14.9
3	Life Support	12
4	Communica	11
5	4th Qtr	1.2
6		

13. Delete the data in row **5** and adjust the range as before to include just the **4** rows. Close the data sheet.

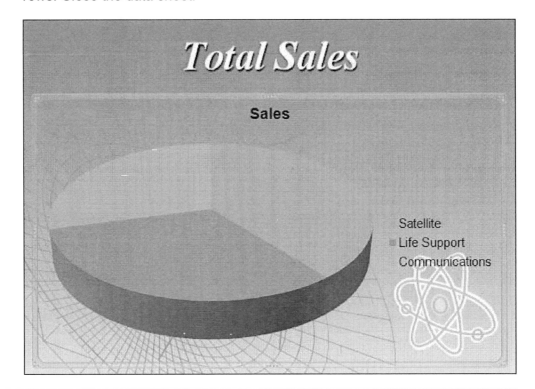

Note: *The clarity and formatting of the chart are poor making it difficult to interpret. This will be addressed in the next exercise.*

14. Save the presentation and leave it open for the next exercise.

Exercise 40 - Formatting Charts

Knowledge:

Fonts and colours of all parts of a chart can be changed.

Activity:

1. In the **objects** presentation, view slide **16**, **Turnover 2**. Click anywhere on the chart to switch to chart edit mode and display the **Chart Tools** (**Design**, **Layout** and **Format** tabs).

2. Holding the cursor over different areas of the chart will display a **ToolTip** which will identify the particular area. Use this to identify the **Plot Area** on the chart.

3. Click on the **Plot Area** to select it and display the **Format** tab.

4. Click ⬛ **Shape Fill** ▾ to display the colour options.

5. Select **Aqua Accent 5** from **Theme Colors**.

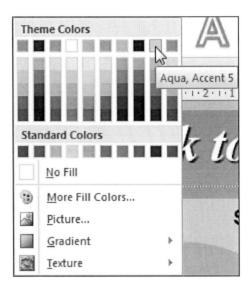

6. Right click on the **2005** data series for any area, e.g. **Satellite**, and select **Format Data Series** from the shortcut menu.

7. Select **Fill** from the left and **Solid fill** from the right. Drop down the **Color** list and change the area colour to **red**, then click **Close**.

8. Click on the word **Satellite** at the bottom of the chart to select the horizontal **Category Axis**.

9. Select the **Home** tab and change the font to **Bold, Italic** and **Dark Blue**.

10. Select the **Legend** at the right of the chart.

11. Set the font to **16pt** and **Dark Blue**.

Exercise 40 - Continued

12. It is also possible to show values on the columns themselves. With the chart still selected, select the **Layout** tab from **Chart Tools**.

13. Click **Data Labels** and select the **Inside End** option.

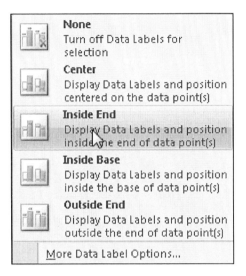

14. Click the **Legend** button. Notice there are options to relocate the legend or not to show it at all. Leave the legend where it is.

15. Display **Total Sales** slide **17**.

16. Click on the pie chart to select it.

17. The chart title of **Sales** is not required. Select the **Chart Tools Layout** tab and click **Chart Title** from the **Labels** group. Select **None** to remove it.

18. The legend on the right is difficult to read and may overlap the graphic. Click on the **Legend** and click and drag the legend border up a little until it clears the underlying graphic (if applicable).

19. To make the legend easier to read, with the **Legend** selected, click **Format** and select **Format Selection** (an alternative to right clicking on the object).

20. Select **Fill** from the left and the **Solid fill** option on the right. Use the **Color** drop-down and select **White**.

21. Close the dialog box and note the results.

22. Save the presentation using the same file name and close it.

Exercise 41 - Develop Your Skills

You will find a *Develop Your Skills* exercise at the end of each Skill Set. Work through it to ensure you've understood the previous exercises.

1. Open the presentation **develop4**, created earlier. If you have not completed the exercise, open the supplied presentation **College4** and save it as **develop4**.

2. Switch to **Slide Master** view, ensure you are looking at the **CollegTemp Slide Master** (use the tooltip to help identify it) and insert the image file **college logo** from the supplied data files.

3. Format the picture to be about **4cm** wide and move it to the top right corner of the slide.

4. Insert the picture **hands.gif**. Make it fit the width of the slide above the footer. Close **Master View**.

5. Insert a new **Title and Content** slide to contain an **Organisation Chart** after slide **4**, **IT Courses**.

6. Give the slide the title **IT Department** and complete the chart using the data below. Create your own names and positions if required.

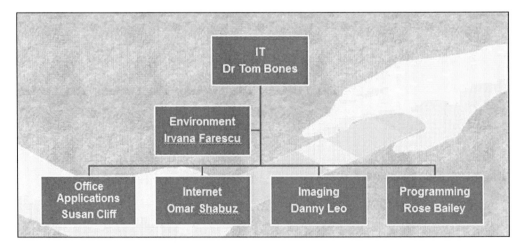

7. Change the font for all text in the chart to **Arial**, **16pt**, **bold**. Change the font colour to **Yellow**.

8. Search the **Clip Art** images using the text **computer**, and insert a suitable image on to slide **4**, **IT Courses**. Do not allow the format of the existing page to be changed.

Exercise 41 - Continued

9.   Format the picture to be about **4cm** wide and move it to the right above the footer.

10.   Repeat this process for slides **6** to **10**, using images relevant to each slide topic.

11.   Insert a new **Title and Content** slide at the end of the presentation. Add a title, **Exam Results**.

12.   Create a **5 x 3** table and enter the data as shown below.

	2002	2003	2004	2005
Pass	81	88	92	95
High Grade	52	64	70	74

13.   Centre the data, horizontally and vertically, in all the cells. Make sure the data values are **bold** and **italic** and the row and column headings are **bold**. Format all the text in the table to be **Dark Blue**.

14.   Move the table to the centre of the slide.

15.   Insert a new slide at the end of the presentation to hold a chart. Add a title of **Chart of Exam Results**.

16.   Create a clustered column chart on the new slide, using data from the slide **11** table in the datasheet.

17.   Format the chart with any colours and fonts to make it more attractive.

18.   Save the presentation as **develop5** and close it.

Note:	*Example solutions are given in the **Answers** section at the end of the guide.*

Summary: PowerPoint Objects

The skills in this Skill Set are concerned with how to create or insert a range of different objects into a presentation. You have inserted an organisation chart as well as Clip Art, pictures, tables and charts.

You have manipulated objects by moving, resizing and deleting. You have also cropped pictures.

Your ITQ evidence must demonstrate the following skills:

- Inserting a wide range of different objects into the presentation:
  - Tables
  - Charts
  - Clip Art
  - Images
  - Photographs

- Manipulating images and other objects within a slide by:
  - Moving and resizing

- Cropping pictures

Skill Set 6

Controlling a Presentation

By the end of this Skill Set you should be able to:

Change Slide Order

Delete and Hide Slides

Use Hyperlinks

Create Action Buttons

Use Preset and Custom Animation

Animate Charts

Set up a Slide Show

Apply Slide Transitions and Timings

Add Sound

Exercise 42 - Changing Slide Order

Knowledge:

To make a presentation flow more smoothly you may want to change the order of some of the slides. **Slide Sorter** view provides an easy way to achieve this.

Activity:

1. Open the **Far North5** presentation and switch to **Slide Sorter** view.

2. Drag the **Zoom** slider, [76% ⊖──────⬚────⊕], at the bottom right of the **Status Bar** to select a zoom level that makes the slide titles legible and shows the maximum number of slides on the screen.

3. Slide **13**, **Department Staff** would be better positioned after slide **4**, **Structure**. Click on slide **13** and hold down the mouse button.

4. Drag the slide towards slide **5** and a line appears as it is moved.

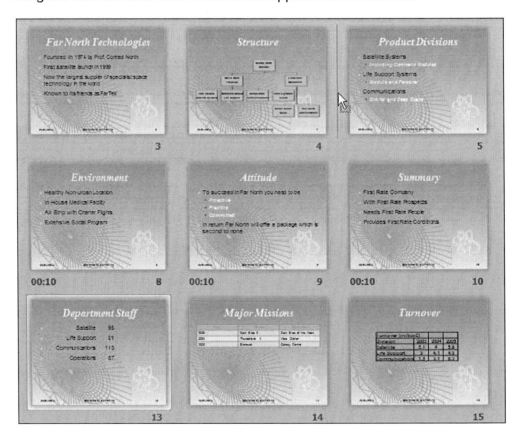

5. When the line is just to the left of slide **5**, release the mouse. The **Department Staff** slide is now slide **5**.

> **Note:** Slides can also be repositioned by using click and drag in the **Slides/Outline** panel on the left of **Normal** view.

6. Save the presentation as **actions** and leave it open.

Exercise 43 - Deleting Slides

Knowledge:

Slides that are no longer required can be deleted. The easiest way to do this is in **Slide Sorter** view.

Activity:

1. In the **actions** presentation, in **Slide Sorter** view, click between slides **3** and **4** and insert a new slide using the **Title and Content** layout.

2. Switch to **Normal** view and enter the title **Our Founder**.

3. Add text to create the following slide:

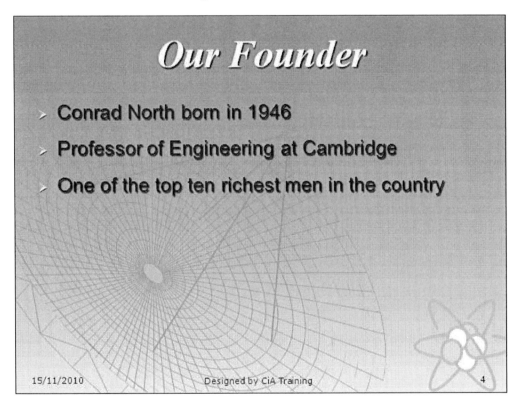

4. The Director has come in to see how the presentation is progressing. He is not happy about the new slide, as he thinks his personal details are not relevant to the presentation. You must delete the slide. Switch to **Slide Sorter** view.

5. Select the slide and then right click to reveal a shortcut menu. Select **Delete Slide** from the menu.

6. He also thinks that slide **13** about the company mascot should not really be part of the presentation. Select that slide in **Slide Sorter** view and press **<Delete>**.

7. Save the presentation using the same file name and leave it open.

Exercise 44 - Hiding Slides

Knowledge:

Occasionally a presentation may have slides that contain additional or sensitive information that does not need to be seen unless specifically requested. If necessary these slides can be hidden.

This feature is particularly useful when a single presentation is to be used for different purposes (i.e. a slide on sales figures can be hidden when giving a presentation to staff, but included when giving the same presentation to managers).

Activity:

1. The Director is still not happy with the presentation. He thinks the slides about turnover should only be displayed when requested, rather than automatically.

2. In the **actions** presentation, in **Slide Sorter** view, select slide **14, Turnover**.

3. Select the **Slide Show** tab and click **Hide Slide**.

4. A symbol appears behind the slide number to indicate that it will be hidden during the slide show.

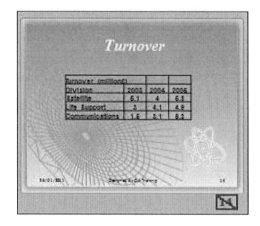

5. Repeat the process to hide slide **15, Turnover 2** and **16, Total Sales**.

6. Select slide **1** and view the slide show, clicking on each slide to advance to the next.

7. Notice that the show now ends with slide **13**.

8. Save the presentation using the same file name and leave it open.

Exercise 45 - Hyperlinks

Knowledge:

Regular users of the Internet will be familiar with **hyperlinks** – text or images that, when clicked, move the user directly to another location. Hyperlinks can be created on slides to navigate to other slides in a presentation, to other files on your computer, or to locations on an Intranet or the Internet.

Activity:

1. In the **actions** presentation, view slide **2**, **A Fresh Career** in **Normal** view.

2. Highlight the text **The Challenge** and select the **Insert** tab and click **Hyperlink**.

3. From the **Insert Hyperlink** dialog box, click the **Place in This Document** button in the left panel then select **10. Attitude** from the list of slide titles.

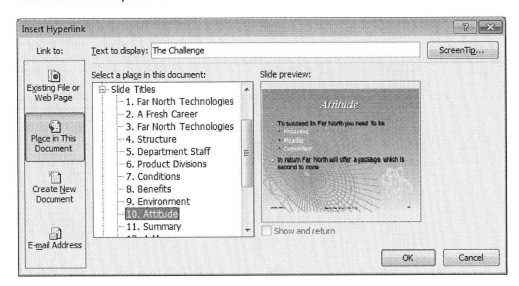

4. Click **OK** to create the hyperlink. The colour of the hyperlink text on the slide is different to other text. When the hyperlink destination has been visited, the text colour will change again.

Note:	*Hyperlink colours are defined in the **Color Scheme** settings.*

5. To test the hyperlink, click the **Slide Show** button, 🖳, at the lower right of the screen with slide **2** still selected.

6. Click on the hyperlink text, **The Challenge**. Instead of moving to slide **3**, the next slide to appear will be slide **10**. Press <**Esc**> to end the slide show.

7. Display slide **2**. Note that the hyperlinked text has changed colour after it has been used.

Exercise 45 - Continued

8. A hyperlink can also be created to reference external information. Highlight the text **The Company**. From the **Insert** tab click the **Hyperlink** button.

9. Select the **Existing File or Web Page** button under **Link to**. Scroll down the list and select **The Company.docx**.

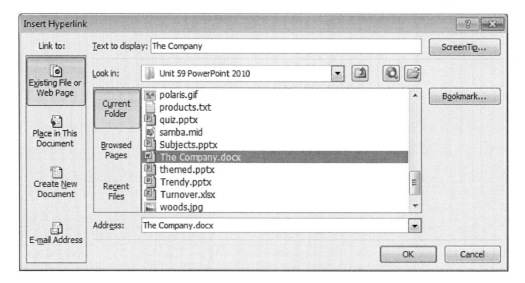

10. Click **OK** to create the hyperlink to this *Word* document.

11. View the slide show, starting from slide **2**.

12. Test the hyperlink by clicking on the text, **The Company**.

13. The *Word* application is opened and **The Company** document is displayed.

14. Close the *Word* application by clicking the **File** tab and then clicking the **Exit** option.

15. *PowerPoint* is displayed again, still viewing the show at slide **2**. Press **<Esc>** to end the show.

16. It has been decided that the hyperlink to the *Word* document is not necessary. Right click on the text, **The Company** and select **Remove Hyperlink** from the shortcut menu. The hyperlink is removed.

17. Save the presentation with same name and leave it open.

Exercise 46 - Action Buttons

Knowledge:

Action buttons are often used to create hyperlinks within a presentation, as an alternative to a text hyperlink. They allow rapid, easy navigation between slides.

Activity:

1. In the **actions** presentation, select slide **13**, **Major Missions**. To add an **Action Button**, click the **Shapes** button on the **Insert** tab. From **Action Buttons** at the bottom of the list, select the **Custom** action button, .

2. Click and drag a rectangular button shape at the bottom left of the slide. The **Action Settings** dialog box appears on the screen.

3. Ensure that the **Mouse Click** tab is selected. Click the **Hyperlink to** option and from the drop-down list, select **Slide**, then from the list of slides displayed, select slide **(14) Turnover** (the hidden slide).

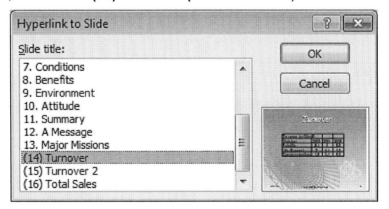

4. Click **OK**, then **OK** again.

> **Note:** *You can draw any shape to use as an action button. Select it and click* **Action** *from the* **Links** *group to display the* **Action Settings** *dialog box, allowing you to select a hyperlink destination. Pictures can also be used as hyperlinks in this way.*

5. With the button still selected, type **Turnover**. This will become the button text. Adjust the size of the button by dragging the corner handles, if required.

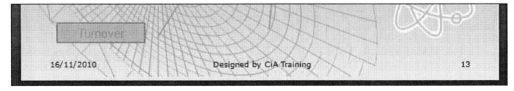

6. Click the **Slide Show** button to see the slide as it will appear in the final presentation. Click the action button.

7. The presentation moves to slide **14**, the **Turnover** slide, even though it is hidden and would not be displayed as part of a normal slide show. Exit the slide show but leave the presentation open.

Exercise 47 - Using Built-In Animation

Knowledge:

Animation can quickly be applied to text and objects on a slide so that they appear on the slide in a variety of different and interesting ways, e.g. fly in, fade, etc.

These effects can be used without having to become involved in the more complex process of defining individual effects.

Activity:

1. Display slide **2** of the **actions** presentation in **Normal** view.

2. Select the **Animations** tab.

3. Select the title text box, **A Fresh Career**, and click the drop-down arrow on the **Add Animation** button.

4. Hover the mouse over each listed effect in turn, to see a preview on the slide.

5. Select the **Fade** effect from the **Entrance** gallery.

6. Now select the bulleted list text box and click the **More** button from the **Animation** group (an alternative). Select **Fly In**

7. Click the **Effect Options** button. The **Direction** can be changed from here, but ensure that the **Sequence** is **By Paragraph**.

> **Note:** *Animation properties such as triggers, timings and sound are included in some schemes but can only be amended by using the **Custom Animation** feature.*

8. Click the **Slide Show** button to see how the presentation looks with the new animation effects. Click the mouse to trigger the next animated text item.

> **Note:** *The **Preview** button on the **Ribbon** can be used to see effects in **Normal** view <u>without</u> clicking the mouse button.*

9. Press <**Esc**> to end the show.

10. Save the presentation and leave it open for the next exercise.

Exercise 48 - Using Custom Animation

Knowledge:

Custom animation allows effects for individual items on a slide to be defined separately. Effects can be chosen from 4 areas. **Entrance effects** (how an item comes on to the screen), **Emphasis effects** (what it does on the screen), **Exit effects** (how an item disappears), and **Motion Paths** (to move an item around a slide). These effects are also known as **builds**.

Customising also allows greater control over details within effects, such as the timing, speed and order of the animations, and any accompanying sound. For any selected effect, all the options can be set from a dialog box with the following tabs:

- The **Effect** tab controls the addition of sounds, what happens to the item after animation, and whether to introduce text all at once, word by word or letter by letter.

- The **Timing** tab controls when an effect is activated – on the click of the mouse or automatically – and how fast the effect runs and whether it repeats.

- The **Text Animation** tab controls how the effects are applied to a bulleted text list (either to the whole list or by heading/subheading).

Activity:

1. In the **actions** presentation, display slide **3**, **Far North Technologies**, in Normal view. From the **Animations** tab, click [Animation Pane]

2. Click on the slide **Title** text box and then open the **Animation** gallery using either method.

3. Select **More Entrance Effects** then select the **Spiral In** effect from within **Exciting**, and then click **OK.**

4. An entry is made, [1 Rectangle 2: F...], in the **Animation Pane** for this slide. Click [Play] to demonstrate the effect and note that it only applies to the title text.

5. Once entered, the effect can be edited. Select the effect in the **Animation** list then click the drop-down arrow to the right and select **Effect Options**.

6. Select the **Effect** tab from the **Spiral In** dialog box (if not already selected).

7. Click in the **Animate text** box and select **By letter**.

8. Click **OK** to apply the amended effect. Notice that the title text now spirals in one letter at a time.

Exercise 48 - Continued

9.   Different effects can be applied to other parts of the slide. Select the main text box (containing the bulleted items).

10. Add an **Entrance** effect of **Dissolve In** (also under **Basic** in **More Entrance Effects**). A new item appears in the **Animation** list.

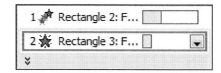

11. Click the drop-down arrow for the new effect and select **Effect Options**.

12. Select the **Text Animation** tab from the **Dissolve In** dialog box.

13. Change the **Group text** option to **As One Object** and click **OK** to view the effect.

14. Select **Effect Options** for this effect again.

15. Select the **Text Animation** tab and change the **Group text** option back to **By 1st Level Paragraphs**.

16. Select the **Timing** tab and change the **Duration** to **2 seconds**.

17. Click **OK** to apply all of these options and view the results. Click **Play** to repeat the preview if required.

> **Note:**   When **Custom Animation** is selected, each item on the slide that has an individual animation effect is given a sequence number which is shown on the slide. Because the current option is to animate text by 1st level paragraphs, each paragraph (line of text) has a different number.

18. Click the 🖳 button in the status bar to see how the effects will appear in an actual presentation. Remember to use mouse clicks to trigger most of the effects. Use <Esc> to terminate the show, when the next slide is displayed.

19. Experiment by trying out some of the different settings within **Effects Options**, and use 🖳 or the **Preview** button to demonstrate the effects.

20. Save the presentation and leave it open.

Exercise 49 - Animating Charts

Knowledge:

Preset Animation Schemes do not apply to inserted objects such as charts, but custom animations can be applied. Animation can be applied to the chart as a whole or to individual elements separately. Available options include:

- How to introduce the chart elements

- Whether or not to animate the grid and legend

- Which animation effect and accompanying sound are applied

- What to do with the chart after it has been animated

Activity:

1. In the **actions** presentation, view slide **15**, **Turnover 2**, in **Normal** view. Select the chart by clicking on it once.

2. Make sure the **Animation Pane** is displayed.

3. Add an **Entrance** effect of **Dissolve In**.

Note:	If **Dissolve In** is not in the gallery, click **More Entrance Effects**, select the effect and click **OK**.

4. By default the animation is applied to the whole chart, as shown by the preview. Click ▶ Play to demonstrate the effect again.

5. Click the arrow to the right of the new animation entry in the **Animation Pane** and select **Effect Options**.

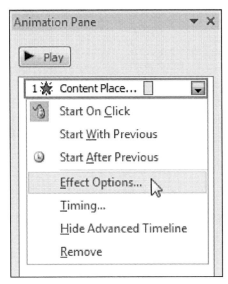

Exercise 49 - Continued

6.   Select the **Chart Animation** tab from the dialog box.

7.   Display the **Group chart** drop-down list and select **By Series**. Make sure **Start animation by drawing the chart background** is checked.

8.   Click **OK** to apply the animation and click  to demonstrate the effect.

> **Note:**   *The slide title should appear. Click once to see the chart background and legend dissolve in. Click again to display all the data for the first category, 2003. The next two clicks will display the data for the 2004 and 2005.*

9.   Press <**Esc**> to end the slide show.

10.   In the **Animation Pane**, select **Effect Options** and then the **Chart Animation** tab again. Select **By Element in Category** and click **OK** to apply the animation.

11.   Click to demonstrate the effect.

> **Note:**   *The slide title should appear. Click once to see the chart background and legend dissolve in. Click again to display the **Satellite** data for **2003**. The next two clicks will display the **Satellite** turnover for the **2004** and **2005**. The next three clicks will show the **Life Support** turnover for the three years in turn, and the next three will show the **Communications** turnover for the three years in turn.*

12.   Press <**Esc**> to end the slide show then close the **Animation Pane**.

13.   Save the presentation and leave it open.

Exercise 50 - Setting Up a Slide Show

Knowledge:

The two most common reasons for creating a presentation are to create a slide show and to produce printed handouts. The slide show can be printed out as slides, projected from the computer on to a screen (with the appropriate equipment), shown on the Internet, or displayed as a show on the computer screen itself. The following exercises demonstrate how to set up the show, with transitions and timings, etc.

Activity:

1. In the **actions** presentation, switch to **Slide Sorter** view.

2. Select the **Slide Show** tab and click **Set Up Slide Show**. The **Set Up Show** dialog box appears.

3. Under **Show slides**, make sure **All** is selected, and select **Manually** under **Advance slides**.

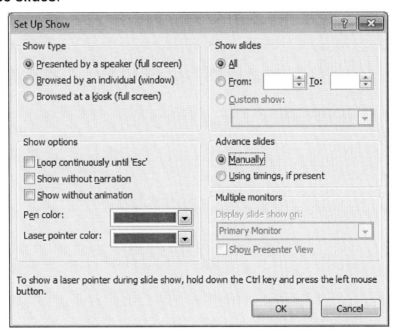

4. Click **OK**.

5. Select the first slide and then click **From Current Slide**. The title slide in the presentation appears.

6. Click the mouse to move to the second slide. Remember some slides have animation effects and you will need to click the mouse button to trigger them. Ignore the hyperlink on slide **2**.

7. Move through the rest of the slide show, activating animations where necessary. Use the action button on slide **13** to navigate to the hidden slides.

8. At the end of the show *PowerPoint* returns to **Slide Sorter** view. Leave the presentation open.

Exercise 51 - Adding Sound

Knowledge:

Sounds can be used in presentations in various ways. A sound can be added to a slide or to an animation effect, so that it plays when the slide is viewed or when the animation is activated. This type of sound is known as a **sound event** and can be played on mouse click (for a single slide) or set to play for the whole presentation.

A voice narration can be recorded to play in a presentation, perhaps if the show was to run on its own without a presenter. Narration takes precedence over other sounds on a slide. You will need a microphone to record and digitise a voice recording, and if you need to edit or cut the sound clip, separate editing software will be required.

Sounds up to 100KB are embedded into a presentation by default, to save space. Large sound files must be stored with the presentation. If the show is presented on a different computer, large sound files must also be installed on that computer. An embedded sound file that is part of the presentation makes the presentation file size much larger. Various formats are supported, e.g. **MIDI**, **MP3**, **.wav** and **.wma** files.

An audio file downloaded or copied from the Internet or from any other source cannot be used in a presentation unless specifically identified by its owner as being copyright-free. Content may be used if the owner has given explicit consent, but in this case it is customary to include a reference to acknowledge the source of the material.

Activity:

1.   In the **actions** presentation, switch to **Normal** view and select slide **15**.

2.   Select the chart and display the **Animation Pane**. Drop down the arrow for the animation and select **Effect Options**.

3.   From the **Effect** tab, drop down the **Sound** options and select **Coin**. Click **OK**. By default, the sound will be added to each introduction of a **Category**.

> **Note:**   *To add individual sounds to each chart column, expand the animation contents, ⊻, and change each effect option from 2-10.*

4.   Display slide **1** in **Normal** view. From the **Insert** tab and the **Media** group, click the **Audio** button.

> **Note:**   *If you click the drop-down on the **Audio** button, select **Audio from File**.*

5.   The **Insert Audio** dialog box is displayed.

6.   Locate the supplied data folder and select the **music.mid** sound file, a copyright free sequence.

7.   Click **Insert**.

Exercise 51 - Continued

8.   The audio icon is displayed on the slide and the **Audio Tools** become available.

9.   Click on **Playback** and, from **Audio Options**, click on the **Start** drop down options and select **Automatically**.

10. Click on the sound icon that appears in the centre of the slide to select it.

11. Display the **Audio Tools Playback** tab.

> **Note:**   **Volume** *can be controlled from the attached speakers, the volume button on the* **Taskbar***, and the* **Volume** *button in the* **Audio Options** *group on the* **Playback** *tab. Make sure that all are on but at a low volume for walkthrough.*

12. Click the **Play** button to play the sound. Make any necessary volume adjustments.

13. Check **Hide During Show** in the **Audio Options** group to hide the sound icon when viewing the slide.

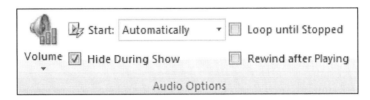

14. View the show now – the sound only plays once.

15. When the sound stops, click to continue viewing the show. Press <**Esc**> to end the show.

16. Select the icon on slide **1** again. Check **Loop Until Stopped** from **Audio Options** on the **Audio Tools Playback** tab. The sound will now repeat while the first slide is on the screen.

17. View the show again and listen for the change in sound.

18. End the show when you are finished.

19. Save the presentation using the same file name, and leave the presentation open for the next exercise.

Exercise 52 - Adding a Movie

Knowledge:

For presentations, the terms video and movie mean the same. Various movie formats are supported by *PowerPoint*, e.g. **asf**, **avi**, **mpeg**, **wmv** files.

As with other materials, a movie file downloaded or copied from the Internet or from any other source <u>cannot</u> be used in a presentation unless specifically identified by its owner as being copyright-free. Content may be used if the owner has given explicit consent, but in this case it is customary to include a reference to acknowledge the source of the material.

Activity:

1. In the **actions** presentation, select slide **3**.

2. Display the **Insert** tab and, from the **Media** group, click the **Video** button.

Note: *If you click the drop-down on the* **Video** *button, select* **Video from File**.

3. The **Insert Video** dialog box is displayed. Locate the supplied data folder and select the **launch.mpeg** movie file, used with the kind permission of **NASA**. Click **Insert**.

4. The video icon is displayed on the slide and the **Video Tools** become available.

5. Click on **Playback** and, from **Video Options**, click on the **Start** drop down options and select **Automatically**.

Note: *The* **Movie Tools Options** *tab will be displayed when a movie is selected.*

6. The movie is placed in the centre of the slide and selected automatically. Move it to the bottom centre of the slide, clear of any text.

7. Click the **Play** button from the **Playback** tab to view the movie.

8. View the show from the beginning – the movie on slide **3** only plays once.

9. When the movie stops, press <**Esc**> to end the show.

10. Save the presentation using the same file name, and leave it open for the next exercise.

Exercise 53 - Applying Slide Transitions

Knowledge:

To make a slide show more interesting, **transitions** can be applied between slides. This is a special effect which controls how one slide changes to the next.

Activity:

1. In the **actions** presentation, display the **Slide Sorter** view.

2. Select the **Transitions** tab. The transition settings are shown in the **Transitions to This Slide** group.

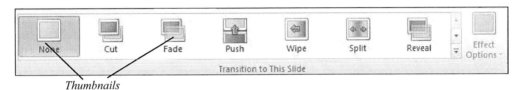

Thumbnails

3. Select slide **2** and then click the **More** button, ⬓, to the right of the transition thumbnails.

4. Select the effect **Flip**, ☐ Flip, from **Exciting.**

5. Under **Advance Slide**, make sure the **On Mouse Click** option checked.

6. Click **Apply To All**, ⬚ Apply To All. The transition effect is now applied to each slide in the presentation. Notice the star icon ▦ beneath each slide that shows a transition has been applied.

> **Note:** If **Apply to All** is not selected, the transition effect will be applied to the selected slide only. Different effects can be applied to different slides.

7. Run the presentation and observe the transition effects between slides.

8. Press <**Esc**> to end the show when you are finished.

9. Save the presentation using the same file name, and leave it open for the next exercise

Exercise 54 - Applying Timings

Knowledge:

Instead of controlling slide shows manually with the mouse, they can be set to run automatically without intervention. If a presentation is run automatically, it can be viewed without the need for a presenter. To do this, the slide transitions must have timings applied to them so that they will move forward at a set pace.

Timings can be applied from the **Timing** area of the **Transitions** tab.

> *Note:*   *If a presentation contains hyperlinks and action buttons it should really be run manually, but for this presentation, timings will be applied.*

Activity:

1.   With the **actions** presentation in **Slide Sorter** view, make sure the **Transitions** tab is displayed.

2.   Under **Advance Slide**, remove the check from the **On Mouse Click** option. Select the **After** option and use the up/down spinner to set the time value to **2** seconds.

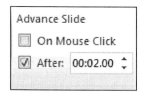

3.   Click **Apply To All**, 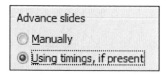, to apply these settings to all slides.

> *Note:*   *This show must be set up to use timings – it currently advances manually.*

4.   Select the **Slide Show** tab and click **Set Up Slide Show**. In the **Set Up Show** dialog box, check that the **Advance slides** is set to **Using timings, if present**.

> *Note:*   *With this option set to **Manually**, the timing settings on the slides would not be used and the mouse would still be needed to advance the show.*

5.   Click **OK**.

6.   View the show. The slides will be displayed automatically in turn, there is no need to click the mouse button.

Exercise 54 - Continued

> **Note:** As the slides are set to advance automatically, any animation effects on a slide will also be activated automatically.

7. The show will run through to the slide **13**. The hidden slides will not be shown as part of the automatic show. If a black slide is shown at the end, click once to return to **Slide Sorter** view.

> **Note:** Timings can be changed for individual slides by selecting the slide, changing the timing value on the **Ribbon**, but <u>not</u> clicking **Apply to All**.

8. Notice how the times for each slide are now shown underneath the slides in **Slide Sorter** view.

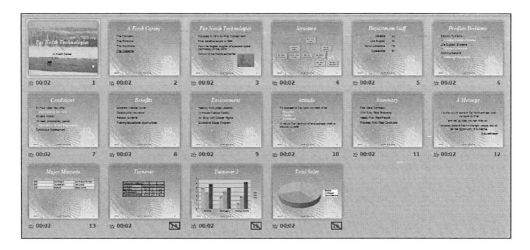

> **Note:** Often an automatic show will be required to run continuously without user intervention.

9. In the **Set Up Show** dialog box, under **Show options**, select the option to **Loop continuously until 'Esc'**.

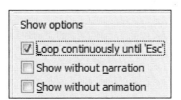

10. Click **OK**, then save the presentation.

11. View the slide show. The slide show will now play automatically, using the timings. When it reaches slide **13**, it will move to the first slide again.

12. Click <**Esc**> at any time to end the show.

13. Close the presentation.

Exercise 55 - Rehearse Timings

Knowledge:

As well as adding timings so that a show can run automatically, timings can be rehearsed so that if a speaker or a recorded sound track is used, then the slides will move on at the appropriate time.

Activity:

1. Open the presentation **Trendy**. Check in **Slide Sorter** view that no timings have been applied.

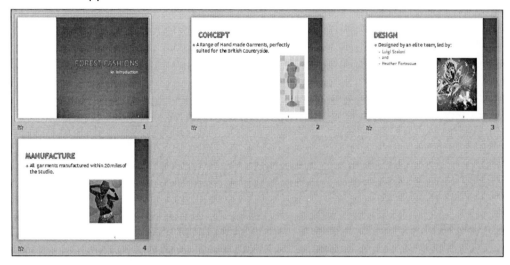

2. Switch back to **Normal** view. To add a sound track across the presentation, display the **Insert** tab and click the **Audio** button.

3. Select **samba.mid** from the supplied data files and click **Insert**.

4. Check **Hide During Show** and **Loop Until Stopped**.

5. In the **Audio Options** group, click the **Start** drop-down and select **Play across slides**.

6. Click on the **Slide Show** tab. In the **Set Up** group, click on **Rehearse Timings**.

7. The slide show starts, with a **Recording** clock in the top corner.

8. Read the content of the slide, and then click the mouse once. The time taken to complete the slide is recorded.

9. The next slide appears and the timer resets, with the total time shown on the right. Once again click the mouse button after the appropriate amount of time has elapsed.

Exercise 55 - Continued

10.   Repeat your rehearsal for the remaining slides.

11.   A dialog box appears showing the total presentation time and asking for confirmation that these times are correct.

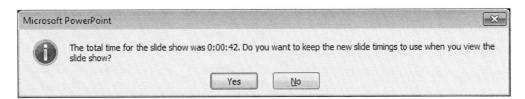

Note:	*Your total time will be different to that shown above.*

12.   Click **Yes** to accept the rehearsed timings.

13.   In **Slide Sorter** view, the timings as rehearsed are shown beneath the slides.

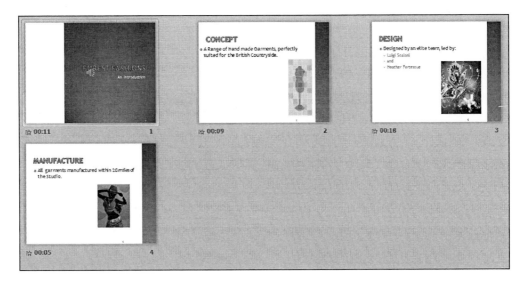

14.   The timings can be edited. Display the **Transitions** tab, and then click on slide **3**.

15.   In the **After** box, use the spinner to change the time to 10 seconds.

16.   View the show using the rehearsed timings.

17.   Close the presentation <u>without</u> saving it.

Exercise 56 - Develop Your Skills

You will find a *Develop Your Skills* exercise at the end of each Skill Set. Work through it to ensure you've understood the previous exercises.

1. Open the presentation **develop5**, created earlier. If you have not created **develop5** then open the supplied presentation **College5** and save it as **develop5**.

2. Move slide **2, College Ethic** to appear after slide **10, Scientific Courses**.

3. The exam result data is now shown on a chart so there is no need to see the original table. Hide the slide with the table (slide **11**).

4. Create a custom action button on slide **12**, the chart, which will link back to slide **11**, the table. Add a title of **Data** to the button.

5. On slide **2 Courses,** create a hyperlink on each of the course names which will link to the appropriate slide for that course.

6. Apply an animation effect of **Wipe** to the title and subtitle on the first slide.

7. On slide **2**, apply a custom animation entrance effect of **Flip** to the bullet points (not the slide title). Edit the effect options so that each line of text is animated separately.

8. Apply an animation effect of **Fly In** to each bulleted item on slide **10**.

9. On slide **12**, the chart, apply a custom animation entrance effect of **Fade** to the chart, not the slide title. Edit the effect options so that the grid and legend are not animated, but each series of data appears separately.

10. Apply a **Slide Transition** effect of **Box** to all slides in the presentation, and set the transition duration to **3** seconds.

11. Set up the show to use a mouse click to advance the slides.

12. View the slide show, using the mouse where necessary.

13. When it is finished, save the presentation as **develop6**.

14. Change the slide transition settings so that the slides advance automatically every four seconds. Change the **Set Up Show** options so that the presentation loops continuously.

15. View the slide show and let it run without using the mouse.

16. Press <**Esc**> to end the show then save the presentation as **develop6a**.

17. Close the presentation.

> **Note:** *Example solutions are given in the **Answers** section at the end of the guide.*

Summary: Controlling a Presentation

The skills in this Skill Set are concerned with how to control the running of a presentation slide show. You have learned how to show slides in a specific order, how to move between slides, and how to change their appearance and transitions during the show.

Your ITQ evidence must demonstrate the following skills:

- Set up a slide show by:
  - Changing slide order
  - Hiding slides
  - Applying slide transitions and timings
  - Using hyperlinks
  - Creating and using Action buttons
  - Adding sound and video

- Deleting slides

- Add preset and custom animation to:
  - Slide text
  - Charts

Skill Set 7

Finishing and Printing

By the end of this Skill Set you should be able to:

Add Speaker's Notes

Create Start and End Slides

Spell check a Presentation

Proof Reading

Print in Portrait and Landscape

Print Slides and Presentations

Print Handouts or Thumbnails

Exercise 57 - Adding Speaker's Notes

Knowledge:

Notes can be added to any or all slides in a presentation. The notes can be to prompt the speaker as he or she runs the slide show, or to give extra information to the audience. Notes can be printed separately, to be handed out to the audience if required.

Activity:

1. Open the **Far North6** presentation from the data files.

2. Display slide **9, Environment**, and select **Notes Page** from the **View** tab.

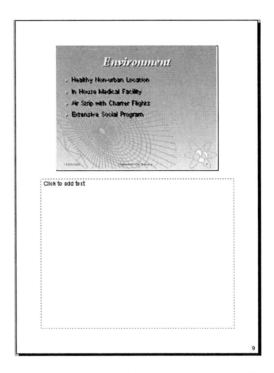

3. Click in the white area beneath the slide and zoom in to **100%**.

4. Type in the following note for the speaker:

   There have been negative comments about the isolation of the location. Try to stress the on-site social life and the quality of the transport links, such as the new road to Drumorden and the flights to many other parts of the country.

5. Scroll down to slide **11** and add the following note, which could give more information to the audience:

   For further information about the job prospects on offer, please collect an Opportunities brochure from the presenter. Anyone wishing to make an application now can do so.

6. Save the presentation as **finished** and switch to **Slide Sorter** view.

Exercise 58 - Start and End Slides

Knowledge:

It is good practice to make sure the audience can easily identify the start and end of a presentation. The start is usually defined by using a **Title Slide**, as has been done in the current presentation. Sometimes a blank or closing slide is used to indicate the end of a presentation – this is particularly useful for manually controlled presentations as it can be left on display as questions are being asked at the end.

Activity:

1. The **finished** presentation should be open in **Slide Sorter** view. It already has a **Title Slide** as slide **1**. Select the last slide, slide **16**.

2. Insert a new, **Title Only** slide.

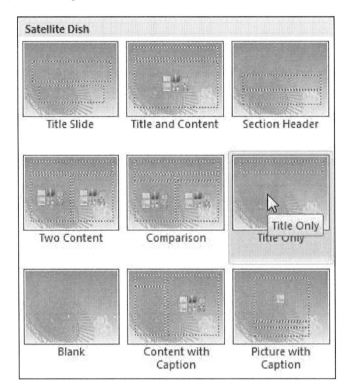

3. Change to **Normal** view. Notice that the graphic and footer information still appear on this slide, as they were added in **Slide Master** view.

4. Add a title of **See you soon at FarTek**.

5. Move the title to the centre of the slide.

6. Save the presentation.

7. Leave the presentation open for the next exercise.

Exercise 59 - Spell Checking

Knowledge:

A presentation should always be checked for spelling mistakes before it is shown to an audience. A spell checking function is available in *PowerPoint*, which can be used to check spelling as text is entered or as a whole presentation.

Note that the spell checker will only highlight words it does not have in its dictionary; it will not find incorrectly used words, e.g. **her** instead of **here**.

Activity:

1. The presentation **finished** should still be open. Make sure the first slide is shown in **Normal** view.

2. Select the **Review** tab and click **Spelling** (or press <F7>). The spell checking process is started.

3. If any spelling errors are detected, alternative spellings will be suggested. You have the option to **Ignore** the suggestion and leave the spelling as it is, or **Change** it to the selected word from the **Suggestions** list.

4. Use the **Ignore** or **Change** buttons as appropriate to correct all errors found in the presentation.

5. When all corrections have been made, click **OK** to end the spell check.

6. Display the last slide of the presentation and add a text box below the title. Enter the text **Aply now!**.

Note: *To create a text box, display the **Insert** menu and select **Text Box** from the **Text** group. On the slide, click and drag to create a box. When you release the mouse button, the text box is created.*

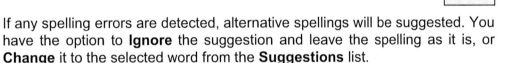

7. The word **Aply** should be underlined in red to indicate a spelling error. Right click on it to see a list of suggested alternatives.

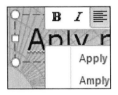

8. Select **Apply** from the list to replace the error.

9. Leave the presentation open for the next exercise.

Note: *PowerPoint 2010 does not have a Grammar Check facility. Because the wording on slides is usually bulleted or phrased, it is not necessary.*

Exercise 60 - Proof Reading

Knowledge:

When a presentation is considered complete, it should be checked thoroughly for accuracy and consistency. Once a presentation is being shown, users will rely on the accuracy of the information in it. Any mistakes can have possibly serious results.

An automated spell checker can help to find spelling mistakes, but you should be aware of its limitations. It will only highlight words it does not recognise from its dictionary. For example, it will not highlight any mistakes in the phrase '**four bedroom detached horse**' because they are all valid words. It is also ineffective when dealing with names and addresses because most real names will probably be detected as spelling mistakes.

Activity:

1. The **finished** presentation should still be open.

2. Display each slide of the presentation in turn and review it carefully, looking for any errors or discrepancies. In particular look out for the following:

    - is the correct word used where there are alternate spellings, e.g. **course** or **coarse**?

    - is the meaning of each slide content clear and accurate, and does it have the meaning you intended?

    - does the overall use of colours present any possible problems (try to consider changing colours that don't allow text or pictures to stand out, or which could prove difficult to read for those with disabilities)?

    - are all objects on the slides, such as images and charts, consistently positioned and sized, and are they clear and relevant?

    - is there any unwanted overlap between objects on a slide, such as images obscuring text?

    - has the text on notes pages been checked for accuracy and meaning?

3. Correct any issues which are discovered and then save the presentation.

4. Leave the presentation open for the next exercise.

Exercise 61 - Page Setup

Knowledge:

Various elements of a presentation can be printed. However, before printing, it may be necessary to change the orientation of the slides or the notes pages/handouts, i.e. from **Portrait** to **Landscape**.

Activity:

1.   In the **finished** presentation, change to **Slide Sorter** view.

2.   Select the **Design** tab and click **Page Setup**.

> **Note:**   *The **Orientation** area can be found to the right of the dialog box.*

3.   Select **Portrait** from the **Slides** group.

> **Note:**   *Slide orientation can also be changed using the **Slide Orientation** button.*

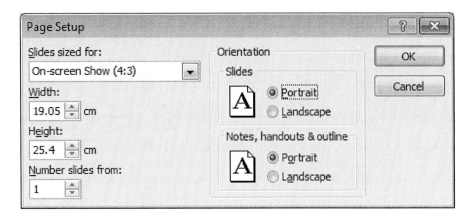

4.   Click **OK** and notice the change to the layout of the slides.

5.   Change the slide orientation back to **Landscape** using the **Slide Orientation** button.

> **Note:**   *Orientation can be changed for notes pages and handouts too.*

6.   Save the presentation, and leave it open for the next exercise.

Exercise 62 - Printing Slides and Presentations

Knowledge:

Slide images can be printed in different forms.

Activity:

1. In **Slide Sorter** view, select slide **15**, click the **File** tab and select **Print**. The **Print** screen appears with a preview of the printed page on the right.

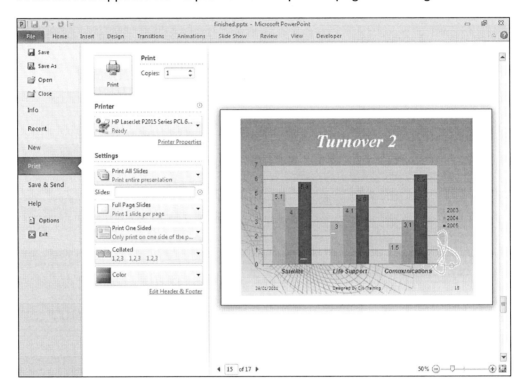

2. Check that the printer is ready to print. If the printer name shown is incorrect, click on the **Printer** drop-down arrow and select the correct one.

3. Click **Print** to print all the slides in the presentation.

4. Display the **Print** screen again. Use the navigation buttons ◄ 10 of 17 ► to display a preview of slide **10**.

5. From the first option on the **Settings range**, drop down the options and select **Print Current Slide** and make sure the **Copies** is set to **1**.

6. From the **Color** drop-down list, select **Pure Black and White**.

7. Click **Print** to print slide **10** only in monochrome.

8. Display slide **15** again. This time print it in **Grayscale** and notice the difference.

9. Leave the presentation open for the next exercise.

Exercise 63 - Other Prints

Knowledge:

As well as slide images, other prints can be produced from the presentation. Handouts can be printed with several slides per sheet (sometimes called **thumbnails**) for an audience to follow as the presentation is running, or the text content of the presentation can be printed in outline form. To aid the presenter, slides can be printed showing speaker's notes.

Activity:

1.   In the **finished** presentation, in **Slide Sorter** view, display the **Print** screen.

2.   Change the first setting to **Print All Slides**.

3.   Display the setting currently showing **Full Page Slides and** select **3 Slides** from the **Handouts** section.

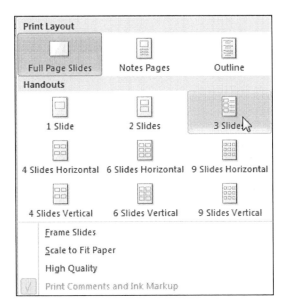

4.   The preview at the right shows how the print out will appear. Click **Print** to print the handouts. At 3 slides per page, an area for written notes is printed alongside each slide image.

5.   Display the **Print** screen again. This time select to print **9 Slides Vertical**.

6.   To print the speaker's notes created earlier, first display the **Print** screen

7.   In the **Slides** box, enter **9-11** and change **9 Slides Vertical** to **Notes Pages**.

8.   Click **Print**.

> **Note:** Changing the **Color** option has the same effect on **Handouts** and **Notes Pages** as it does for printing slides.

9.   Save and then close the presentation.

Exercise 64 - Develop Your Skills

You will find a *Develop Your Skills* exercise at the end of each Skill Set. Work through it to ensure you've understood the previous exercises.

1. Open the presentation **develop6**, created earlier. If you have not created **develop6**, open the supplied presentation **College6** and save it as **develop6**.

2. Add the following speaker's notes:

    Slide **2**:-   **New courses to be announced for next year include: Media Studies and Fashion.**

    Slide **5**:-   **Many of our courses can be used towards the ABC qualification.**

3. Spell check the presentation, making the appropriate changes.

4. Create a blank slide at the end of the presentation.

5. Hide the **Background Graphics** for the new slide only and insert the **college logo** image.

6. Resize the logo to **17cm** high and centralise it on the slide so that it does not obscure the footer.

7. Check that all the footers are uniform, making any adjustments.

8. Check all slides and make adjustments so that no text or pictures overlap. This may be done in **Slide Master** or on individual slides.

9. Print the presentation as **Notes Pages** in portrait orientation.

10. Print handouts, **3** to a page.

11. Save the presentation as **complete**.

12. Close the presentation.

13. Close *PowerPoint*.

Note: *A copy of the final version of the presentation developed in the **Develop Your Skills** exercises in this guide can be found with the supplied data files. The file is named **College Complete**.*

Summary: Finishing and Printing

The skills in this Skill Set are concerned with how to finish off a presentation and how to produce output from it in various forms.

<u>Your ITQ evidence must demonstrate the following skills:</u>

- Add Start and End Slides

- Spell check presentations

- Use proof reading techniques to check that text and images look professional

- Use Page Setup to prepare for printing:
    - Print in Portrait and Landscape

- Print:
    - Slides
    - Presentations
    - Handouts or thumbnails

- Add and print speaker notes

ITQ Assessment Criteria

B1	**Input and combine text and other information within presentation slides**	
1.1	Identify what types of information are required for the presentation	☐
1.2	Enter text and other information using layouts appropriate to the type of information	☐
1.3	Insert charts and tables into presentation slides	☐
1.4	Insert images, video or sound to enhance the presentation	☐
1.5	Identify any constraints which may affect the presentation	☐
1.6	Organise and combine information from different sources for presentations	☐
1.7	Store and retrieve presentation files effectively, in line with local guidelines and conventions where available	☐
B2	**Use presentation software tools to structure, edit and format slide sequences**	
2.1	Identify what slide structure and themes to use	☐
2.2	Select, change and use appropriate templates for slides	☐
2.3	Select and use appropriate techniques to edit slides and presentations	☐
2.4	Select and use appropriate techniques to format slides and presentations	☐
2.5	Identify what presentation effects to use to enhance the presentation	☐
2.6	Select and use animation and transition effects appropriately to enhance slide sequences	☐
B3	**Prepare a slideshow for presentation**	
3.1	Describe how to present slides to meet needs and communicate effectively	☐
3.2	Prepare a slideshow for presentation	☐
3.3	Check a presentation meets needs, using IT tools and making corrections as necessary	☐
3.4	Identify and respond to any quality problems with presentations to ensure that presentations meet needs	☐

Evidence Requirements

OCR has defined **Evidence Requirements** to meet the ITQ Assessment Criteria provided on the previous page. A complete evidence checklist must be submitted with every unit to ensure all evidence required for the assessment and achievement of this unit has been produced.

> **Note:**   *This unit has a credit value of 4 and can be achieved by completing as many different tasks as you feel are necessary.*

B1   *Input and combine text and other information within presentation slides*

B2   *Use presentation software tools to structure, edit and format slide sequences*

Create a presentation of a minimum of six slides with four different types of information including images, text, audio/video using a range of tools and techniques and identifying any constraints on the use of any of the information within the slides. Save the presentation appropriately.

B3   *Prepare a slideshow for presentation*

Provide evidence of your final presentation. This must show evidence of at least one animation, one slide transition and at least three different types of format.

Sample Scenarios

These suggested tasks are designed to help you develop your own ideas, which should be relevant to your own workplace (or workplace simulation). You could produce something similar to the suggestions below. *Please note that each task may not cover all evidence required for the unit in its own right.* Make sure that you obtain printouts and screen shots as you are creating your own presentations, so that they can be used as ITQ evidence.

The presentations used in the course of this guide could all be adapted to be suitable types of task for this unit. Examine them to see if you could use the ideas within them to create your own solutions. It is essential that these examples are only used to show the sort of tasks that could be used. They must not be submitted in their own right.

Company Product:

Create a continuously running presentation which promotes and explains a company product. This could highlight key benefits of the product, describe how the product works, suggest when and where it could be used, and display details of the costing structure including any introductory offers. Such a presentation would probably make a lot of use of images and animations.

Company Induction:

Create an induction presentation for new starters to your company/organisation. This could include slides describing various departments, pictures of key staff, and details of pension schemes, social clubs, etc. It could also be a place to display some of the key conditions of employment and any rules and instructions peculiar to your company/organisation. It would be useful for such a site to have a comprehensive system of hyperlinks and bookmarks so that users can easily access the areas that interest them.

Training Course:

Create a presentation to summarise a training or teaching course that you are running. Include the aims and key features of the course, and details of the individual topics covered. Other items which could be put into the presentation include background information which could be displayed only where required and a list of potential discussion points. By including comprehensive speakers' notes, the presentation could be printed out as handouts and used as a useful set of notes to accompany the course.

Answers

The images given here are provided mainly to show the layout of the presentations developed in this guide at various stages.

Exercise 14

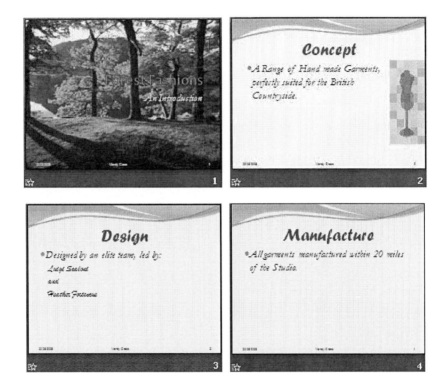

Exercise 20

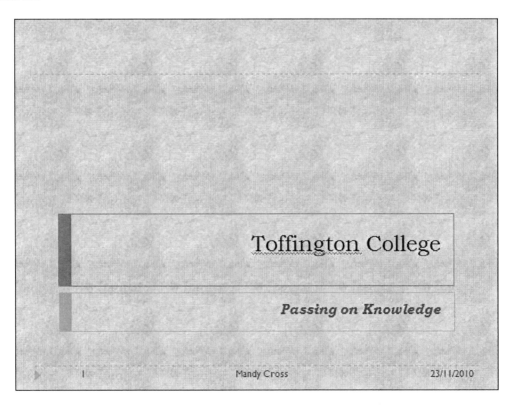

Exercise 27

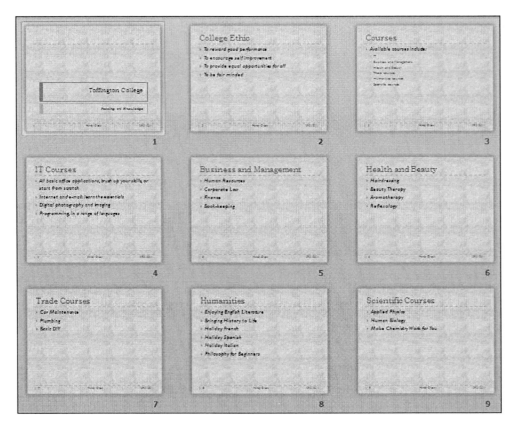

Exercise 41

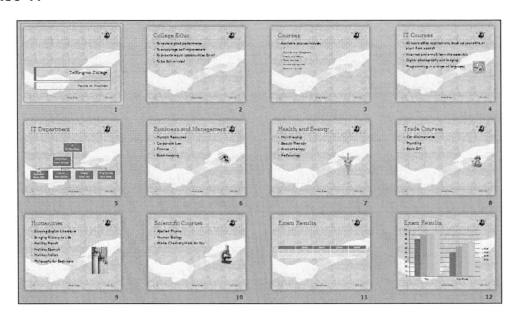

Exercise 56

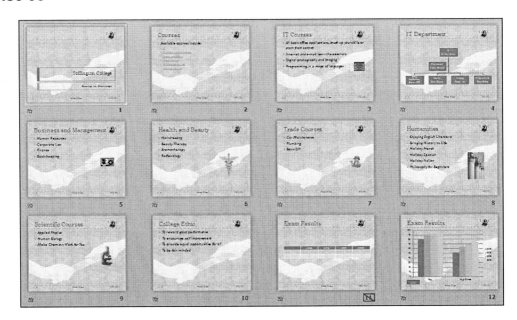

Glossary

Alignment	The arrangement of text or objects in relation to a slide or text box, e.g. left, centre, right, top, bottom.
Animation	Special effects which make text and other objects appear to move on screen.
Background	The colour or graphic behind the contents of the slide.
Bullet Levels	Used to emphasise major and minor points.
Copy	Create a duplicate of an object or text. Used when the copied item is to be duplicated.
Custom Animation	Applying animation effects to individual objects on a slide and specifying their operation.
Cut	Remove an object or text. Used when the cut item is to be moved somewhere else.
Footer	Text or numbers appearing at the bottom of the slide, notes page or handout.
Header	Text or numbers appearing at the top of the slide, notes page or handout.
House Style	A collection of style guidelines used by an organisation to ensure all published materials match their corporate image. Generally includes fonts, logos and colours to use.
Object	Any item on a slide, e.g. a drawn shape, image, chart, text box, etc.
Orientation	Which way up the slide/handout is: **Portrait** or **Landscape**.
Paste	Used after **Cut** or **Copy** to position the item (move or duplicate).
Presentation	A collection of slides used by a speaker as a visual aid.
Slide Layout	The type of slide, e.g. **Title and Content**, **Title Only**
Slide Master	This view is for adding items that are to appear on all slides in a presentation.
Slide Show	A preview of the presentation, with all effects, sounds, etc.
Text Effects	Formatting such as bold, italic, shadow, superscript.
Timings	Govern how long an item or slide remains on screen during a show.
Transition	How one slide moves to the next.
Views	Different ways of looking at slides.

Index

Other Products from CiA Training

CiA Training is a leading publishing company which has consistently delivered the highest quality products since 1985. Our experienced in-house publishing team has developed a wide range of flexible and easy to use self-teach resources for individual learners and corporate clients all over the world.

At the time of publication, we currently offer materials for:

- **ITQ Level 1, Level 2 and Level 3**

- **New CLAIT, CLAIT Plus and CLAIT Advanced**

- **ECDL Syllabus 5.0**

- **ECDL Advanced Syllabus 2.0**

- **Start IT**

- **Skill for Life in ICT**

- **Functional Skills ICT**

- **CiA Revision Series**

- **Open Learning Guides**

- **Trainers Packs with iCourse Professional**

- **And many more...**

Previous syllabus versions are also available upon request.

We hope you have enjoyed using this guide and would love to hear your opinions about our materials. To let us know how we're doing and to get up to the minute information on our current range of products, please visit us at:

www.ciatraining.co.uk

Notes